COUNCIL-MANAGER
GOVERNMENT

The Political Thought
of Its Founder,
Richard S. Childs

COUNCIL-MANAGER GOVERNMENT

The Political Thought of Its Founder, Richard S. Childs

By JOHN PORTER EAST

THE UNIVERSITY OF NORTH CAROLINA PRESS
Chapel Hill

To my wife, Sis,
without whom nothing
would be possible

Acknowledgments

This study took initial form as a doctoral dissertation at the University of Florida, and I am indebted to the entire Department of Political Science at that institution. This includes Professor Manning J. Dauer, Chairman of the Department, and all of his staff under whom I have done graduate work. I am indebted to Professors John M. DeGrove and Arthur W. Thompson for their suggestions in the preparation of the manuscript and for their courtesy in giving the task top priority in their crowded schedules. Moreover, I found exceedingly rewarding their respective courses in urban government and politics and American thought and culture. This study is built considerably upon the foundation that I obtained in those courses.

To Richard S. Childs, the subject of this book, I acknowledge deep appreciation. He gave generously of his interest and time, and he co-operated readily in responding to the many requests with which I badgered him. During my interview with him in January, 1964, in New York City, he opened up his apartment to my wife and me and entertained us regally and graciously. His attitude and personal courtesies have made this undertaking a pleasure.

To the United States Government I acknowledge a debt of gratitude for the National Defense Education Act Fellowship that enabled me to pursue graduate training culminating in this book.

To Miss Charlotte Isbill, who typed the manuscript, I offer sincere thanks, for she is a craftsman who takes extreme pride in her work.

I owe my greatest debt to Professor Gladys M. Kammerer, who served as Chairman of my dissertational committee when this study was initially undertaken. I conceived the possibility of doing this study while I was a student in her stimulating courses in public administration. It is a considerable intellectual debt that I owe, and her suggestions and insights pervade the entire book. However, my debt to her runs beyond the form and substance of this final product. Her kindness in giving unstintingly of her time from her demanding schedule to examine the manuscript is something for which I am deeply grateful. Her insistence upon vigorous and original thinking, and her insistence upon quality and disdain of the shoddy has already returned rich dividends to me.

I am indebted to my mother and father, who have always stressed the importance of the pursuit of excellence in education, and who have, unlike many parents, always encouraged their children to go where their talents and interests led them.

I am grateful to East Carolina College for the reduced teaching load, which enabled me to prepare the manuscript in final form.

Finally, I offer my gratitude to my wife and children, for their quiet suffering while I neglected them in preparation of this book.

Contents

COUNCIL-MANAGER
GOVERNMENT

The Political Thought
of Its Founder,
Richard S. Childs

I

Introduction

"For there is such a thing as political science although the lawyers and politicians who design city governments rarely realize it."
Richard S. Childs, 1910[1]

The American municipal reform movement was a sweeping reaction to the "bossism" and "machine politics" that had grown steadily in scope and influence during the industrial-urban transformation that followed the Civil War. The nature of the municipal reform movement and the conditions of urban political life against which it represented a countervailing movement are examined in detail in the succeeding chapter. The fact to be emphasized at this point is that though manifested in various forms, in general the reform movement sought to oust the spoilsmen and to return the government of American cities to "the people."

1. Richard S. Childs, "What Ails Pittsburgh?" *American City*, III (July, 1910), 9.

The definitive study of this movement has not yet been produced, but when it is, conceivably Richard Spencer Childs may stand in the forefront as the principal figure. To date he has labored over a half century for municipal reform, but this is only a quantitative factor, which alone could not insure historical prominence. Vastly more important is the qualitative element. Consistently since 1909 Childs has been a prolific writer in the cause of urban reform, as well as an indefatigable agitator and promoter. The impressive statistical result of his efforts is the adoption of council-manager government, Childs's primary contribution to municipal reform, in roughly one-half of the nation's cities of over ten thousand population, which total includes nearly one-fourth of the American population. Although now in his eighty-third year, Childs still carries on his reformist activities from the National Municipal League offices in New York City.

Childs was born on May 24, 1882, the son of William Hamlin and Nellie Spencer Childs. His father, a highly successful financier and businessman, was a reformer in his own right, and his impact upon his son is clear, as the ensuing chapter will reveal. Though born in Manchester, Connecticut, Childs since early boyhood has counted New York City as home. He attended preparatory school in Brooklyn and was graduated from Yale in 1904, when he began a long business career. He started this career as an advertising executive with the Erickson Company and moved on to become general manager of the Bon Ami Company, founded by his father, and later assistant to the president of A. E. Chew Company. Ultimately he became executive vice president of the Lederle Laboratories, a position that he held from 1935 to 1944, and from 1929 until his retirement from private business activity in 1947, he served as a director of the American Cyanamid Company. Despite this long and demanding commitment to private corporate endeavors (not to mention the family demands of bringing up two daughters), Childs carried on tirelessly his avocation and first love, the cause of municipal reform. Since 1947, as Chairman of the Executive Committee of the National Municipal League, he has been able to convert this avocation into a vocation, though he serves without remuneration. In his words, he is now having "the most fun in my life."[2]

Unlike most municipal reformers, Childs has constructed an ideal model of municipal government. This model is based on a body of doctrine itself based essentially on conventional wisdom. Increasingly in recent years, within the discipline of political science, has arisen the "behavioral persuasion." This newer approach has precipitated in the study of urban government and politics a tough-minded empirical testing of municipal reform doctrine, which to a considerable extent is doctrine developed by Childs. In the study of urban politics the result has been a collision between what are sometimes dubbed the "old" and the "new" political sciences. Childs is an excellent point of departure for bringing this conflict into focus. The underlying hypothesis of this study is that this conflict is not imaginary or minor, but, on the contrary, is a real, significant, and deep-seated one that may be irreconcilable. In the final analysis it is the nature and

2. Quoted in "The Idea Grew," *National Municipal Review*, XL (January, 1951), 63.

ramifications of this conflict that are the principal concerns of this study.

This conflict arises from differences in approach to the study of the world of politics. Childs is preoccupied in his model building with the formal and structural elements of government. His approach is a prescriptive one and is lodged basically in a priori assumptions. With these orientations, Childs has proceeded to construct a highly systematic and rationalistic "machine model" of municipal government. As contended in the following chapters, in this approach Childs reflects many of the intellectual currents of his earlier years, including pragmatism, Progressivism, scientific management, the "principles approach," and the "organizational-chart approach."

Aside from the erection of a model for urban government, there is a further crucial element of the Childs scheme and approach which is explored extensively. This matter is the striking fact that Childs's system is closed. This statement means that his value theories are unaccompanied by causal theories and the subsequent empirical testing that these latter theories entail. Not only does Childs himself decline to test his ideal type empirically, but, in substance, he does not adjust his model to the empirical findings of other students. It is the underlying hypothesis of Chapter IV that Childs lacks this causal theory because of his conception of the worlds of politics and administration. This is a formal, static, and rationalistic view in which there is no need for causal theories to test the ideal schema's adjustment to "political realities." In this conception Childs depicts the phenomena of politics and administration as not primarily matters of continuing change and process;

consequently, his system of statics does not demand theories of testing, for there is simply nothing to test. In short, in the Childs view "the ideal" and "the real" are virtually the same; therefore, theories which might reveal incongruities between the two are not required, and, as a further consequence, the ideal model becomes applicable in all political settings.

Childs's approach is anathema to those of the "behavioral persuasion." This latter school seeks a scientific basis for the study of politics. In Eulau's words, "The behavioral persuasion in politics aspires to the status of science,"[3] and, in contrast to the Childs approach, it is predominantly descriptive rather than prescriptive. Dahl has written, "Thus the 'behavioral approach' might better be called the 'behavioral mood' or perhaps even the 'scientific outlook.' "[4] The choice of the word *mood* is an apt one, for the significant fact is the general orientation of the "new" political science with its emphasis upon the discovery of the "realities"—the "is"—of the political realm. To ascertain the "is" the mood is decidedly empirical, and the ultimate hope is to build "A science of politics which deserves its name ... [built] from the bottom up ... by the slow, modest, and piecemeal cumulation of relevant theories and data."[5] This approach is at odds with the a priori one of Childs in which political theories are constructed from the top down.

The conflict between the behavioral and the Childs approaches is sharpest regarding the matter of the

3. Heinz Eulau, *The Behavioral Persuasion in Politics* (New York: Random House, 1963), p. 111.
4. Robert Dahl, "The Behavioral Approach," *American Political Science Review*, LV (December, 1961), 768.
5. Eulau, *Behavioral Persuasion*, p. 9.

closed system. In contrast with Childs the behavioralists perceive, in the tradition of Bentley,[6] of political
and administrative phenomena as largely processual
matters, and, consequently, they have a compelling
need for vigorous causal theory. This theory calls for
the framing of hypotheses about political behavior
and testing these hypotheses in the field with the most
advanced techniques that behavioral science can offer.
The behavioralists reject the closed system effect of
the Childs scheme because of the eye-opening impact
of their empirical testing, and they refuse to accept
the Childs premise that "the ideal" and "the real"
are virtually identical. On the contrary, they submit
empirical studies that conclude that there are often
wide gaps between the supposed operation of the
ideal model and the actuality. The behavioralists submit that frequently the effect of this disparity is to
ensnare in serious inconsistencies a traditionalist
model builder of Childs's type. The inconsistencies
are said to arise from the fact that while the model
builder may profess that his schema produces one set
of values, in reality it may be that his model is in
fact destructive of those ends or at least is producing
effects not originally envisioned or desired. To those
of the "behavioral mood" the inconsistency results
from the failure of the traditionalist to test his model
empirically in the field and to adjust it to the realities
that such testing reveals. These critical matters are
examined in Chapter V.

The "behavioral persuasion" collides with the
Childs contention that the ideal type has universal applicability. As hypothesized in the concluding chap-

6. Arthur F. Bentley, *The Process of Government* (Bloomington,
Indiana: Principia Press, 1949).

ter, this divergence stems also principally from the fact that Childs in his conception of politics and administration has no requirement for causal theory, while the behavioralists and their intellectual kin in their conception of these matters have a strong need for rigorous and sophisticated empirical testing. To Childs, who has no causal theory to indicate otherwise, "the ideal" and "the real" become nearly coterminous; consequently, he believes that his model has universal validity in all political settings irrespective of time and varying local conditions. In contrast, supported by a maturing causal theory, the behavioral approach finds that the validity of the model will vary greatly from community to community depending upon the operative variables.

Because the greatest importance of Childs lies in his development of a model and its supporting doctrine, both of which have been widely accepted, these contributions by Childs are the primary concern of this analysis. There are, however, other facets of Childs's extensive activity that warrant passing comment. For example, it is known that Childs has preached reformism to the rest of the nation, but it is probably less well known that he has practiced his preachments in his own city. From 1928 to 1940, Childs was president of the City Club of New York, which is a nonpartisan group dedicated to ending the rule of Tammany Hall through the rise of "honest, efficient, municipal government."[7] From 1943 until 1950 he served as chairman of the Citizens Union, which is, similar to the City Club, "a union of citizens,

7. Frank M. Stewart, *A Half Century of Municipal Reform: The History of the National Municipal League* (Berkeley: University of California Press, 1950), p. 13.

without regard to party, for the purpose of securing the honest and efficient government of the city of New York,''[8] and, it should be added, for the purpose of undermining the Tammany machine, Childs's eternal bête noire.

Childs has not, however, confined his New York City civic activities to the scope of these organizations. On the contrary, he is too distrustful of political organizations, and too impetuous and spirited, to be so limited. His efforts in New York have ranged from ''everything that could hurt Tammany Hall''[9] to urging the City's acceptance of the council-manager plan.[10] It is revealing that on Childs's eightieth birthday, May 24, 1962, Mayor Robert Wagner proclaimed, ''The City of New York is eternally grateful to you for making yourself available whenever the need arose for your splendid talents and counsel.''[11] Similar tributes came from such famous New Yorkers as Governor Nelson Rockefeller, Senator Jacob Javits, and the late Governor and Senator Herbert H. Lehman.[12]

In the following chapter, reasons are adduced to explain the fact that generally Childs has directed his reform efforts to the municipal scene. However, to afford a further outlet for his energy, Childs has ventured off into other areas of civic concern. For example, at the present time he is carrying on a ''one-man war'' to change the coroner's office from an elective ''lay-politico'' one to one filled by an appointive

8. Slogan appearing on the letterhead of the organization.
9. Letter to the author, March 10, 1964.
10. A perusal of the *New York Times Index* will give a quantitative indication of Childs's civic endeavors in New York.
11. *New York Times*, May 25, 1962, p. 25, col. 5.
12. *Ibid.*

qualified medical examiner.[13] Furthermore, he is interested in perfecting a mechanically sound model state presidential primary law, as well as in continuing to produce a compendium on legislative apportionment to serve as an "arsenal" in the struggle against malapportionment.[14] In this latter endeavor, of course, he is indirectly looking after the interests of his urban people.

Childs's activity in national partisan politics has been negligible. With roots in Progressivism generally and the Progressive Party in particular, he has, except for a vote for Wilson in 1916, voted consistently for the Republican presidential candidate. Today Childs's Republicanism is that of the "liberal" wing. His national political preferences lie with the Rockefeller-Javits brand of Republicanism rather than with the Goldwater-Tower variety.[15]

Although he has not written extensively on the subject, he has displayed in the field of foreign affairs a keen interest in and support of the League of Nations, and in more recent years he has shown similar attitudes regarding the United Nations and a powerful World Court.[16]

These peripheral items are not injected for discussion in this introduction merely to "round out the

13. The quotations are taken respectively from two unpublished manuscripts by Childs: Richard S. Childs, "Twelfth Annual Report of the Guest Artist," November, 1959, p. 1 (typed manuscript); "Best States for a Murder," October, 1963, p. 1 (mimeographed).

14. The quotation is taken from Childs, "Twelfth Annual Report of the Guest Artist," p. 1.

15. Recently Childs wrote, "I am instinctively hostile to Barry Goldwater and like Rockefeller. If Kennedy had been candidate for president next November, however, I would have voted for him, I expect, instead of any Republican." Letter to the author, March 10, 1964.

16. For example, see *New York Times*, February 4, 1945, p. 8, col. 7; March 9, 1945, p. 18, col. 6.

story.'' They are included at this point for the perspective they afford. For a man of more modest
talents they might represent a total productivity, but
for Childs they represent only a respite from the
central task of promoting adoption of the council-
manager plan of government, and its accompanying
doctrine, by all of the cities in America.

In transporting throughout the country what he
considers a ''revolution,'' Childs has employed as his
major organizational vehicle the National Municipal
League, which has been described as ''the inspiration
and chief counsel for most of the civic reform movement in this century in the United States.''[17] He
served as president of the League from 1927 to 1931,
and, as noted, since 1947 he has held the office of chairman of the Executive Committee. In addition to hold-
ing office, Childs has been throughout the years a
strong supporter of the League and one of its stanchest
financial backers.[18] But to relate in detail the history
of the relationship between him and the League would
go wide of the mark in an attempt to understand the
genuine core of Childs's thought.[19] To accomplish
this latter task, the political scientist must return to
the Childs model of municipal government and its
supporting doctrine, and it is with these matters that
this study is principally occupied.

Aside from reading numerous secondary works, to
ascertain the ''real'' Childs I immersed myself in the
corpus of his writings. In addition to his two books,
Short Ballot Principles and *Civic Victories: The*

17. Quoted in Alfred Willoughby, ''R. S. Childs,'' n.d., p. 3
(mimeographed).
18. Stewart, *Municipal Reform*, p. 187.
19. For a history of the League which includes, of course, facts
relating to Childs's participation, see *ibid.*, *passim*.

Story of an Unfinished Revolution,[20] Childs has produced over the past half century nearly one hundred published articles, not to mention extensive pamphlet material disseminated by the National Short Ballot Organization and the National Municipal League. In addition, Childs made available to me his personal files and extensive collections of memorabilia. After intensive exposure to these materials, the substance of Childs's thought began to take form. To corroborate my materials and to fill in data, I had the good fortune to spend relaxed hours in Mr. Childs's New York City apartment, and in his League office, conducting an open-end interview in which my subject permitted me to probe deeply. In addition to the substantive information it afforded, this interview, to use the lawyer's jargon, allowed me to learn much from "the demeanor of the witness."

Because Childs and his father, who died in 1928, have lived so many years in New York City, I have found that the *New York Times* (microfilm) offered a rich lode of biographical material on both men. Childs is a distinguished New Yorker, as was his father before him, and the *Times* covers his activities accordingly. Childs made available to me his copy of the privately printed biography of his father. This volume, entitled *William Hamlin Childs,* was written by Childs in 1957, and it, too, afforded valuable biographical data.

Less fruitful were my inquiries to various personalities who have known and worked with Childs over the years. For the most part, the responses were prompt and encouraging; however, there was little

20. (Boston: Houghton Mifflin Co., 1911); (New York: Harper and Brothers, 1952).

that these persons were able to add to an understanding of Childs's philosophy that was not already available to me. The respondents frankly conceded this state of affairs, and mainly they simply reaffirmed their great admiration for him. In addition, the Library of Congress provided microfilm copies of communications which Childs and his father had with Woodrow Wilson. With regard to substantive information, these materials also contributed little; however, they did serve to corroborate the close relationship that existed between Childs and Wilson in the National Short Ballot Organization.

It was from this broad cast of the net that I was able to construct the Childs model, with its supporting doctrine, and to delineate its foundations. From these endeavors emerged my perception of Childs. In the critique of the model, I have drawn heavily upon the thinking and empirical studies of the "new" political scientists of "the behavioral persuasion." As will be evident to those who persist to the end, this intellectual debt is a heavy one.

II

The Foundations of Childs's Philosophy

"For the American people—you and I—do want good government. And we shall have it yet!" Richard S. Childs, 1910.[1]

In Chapter III we turn to a consideration of the construction of the Childs model and its supporting doctrine; however, before that task can be undertaken it is essential to examine the foundations of Childs's thinking. In the case of Childs this effort is particularly rewarding because he reflects much of the intellectual environment of the early decades of this century. In the first section that follows, the purpose is to place Childs within the ferment of the pragmatic and Progressive revolt and to show further that his

1. Richard S. Childs, "Politics Without Politicians," *The Saturday Evening Post*, CLXXXII (January 22, 1910), 35.

attitudes have been conditioned considerably by urbanism and its frequent companion, machine politics. The second section is concerned with specific intellectual currents that have influenced Childs's thought. The basic current is the scientific management school, and from it flows the "principles approach" and the "organizational-chart approach." Admittedly there is artificiality in dividing the philosophical composition of an era into tidy categories such as "Progressivism" and "scientific management." Yet, if one is aware that these categories are not "real" in themselves but only aids in the search for reality, then the approach has defensible heuristic value.

The final section deals with the short ballot movement, which is, although not technically a "foundation" of Childs's philosophy, a highly significant phase of his life mirroring remarkably the intellectual trends analyzed in the following two sections.

The Ideological Setting

Pragmatism and Progressivism

Pragmatism, often considered America's original contribution to philosophy, sprang to life in the period after the Civil War through the contributions of Charles Peirce, Chauncey Wright, William James, and ultimately of course, John Dewey. Richard Hofstadter has observed, "pragmatism, which, in the two decades after 1900, rapidly became the dominant American philosophy, breathed the spirit of the Progressive era."[2] It is beyond the scope of this study to

2. Richard Hofstadter, *Social Darwinism in American Thought* (Boston: The Beacon Press, 1955), p. 123.

attempt an analysis of pragmatism in all of its sub-
tleties and nuances; however, this peculiarly American
philosophy possesses certain fundamental tenets that
are basic to an understanding of Progressivism
generally and to an understanding of the political philosophy of Richard S. Childs in particular.

In part pragmatism was a reaction to the Spence-
rian determinism of the Gilded Age. The pragmatists
rejected the determinism of Spencer and the social
and economic predestination of Sumner and believed
it was possible for *man* "to direct the struggle." The
mood of pragmatism was iconoclastic, experimental,
and empirical. It rejected a notion of absolute
"truth" with a capital *T* and accepted a world of
loose ends. This philosophy, with its acceptance of
flux and change, with its emphasis upon man and his
ability to manipulate his environment and direct his
own destiny, fed the spirit of reform of the Progressive years. Henry Steele Commager concludes that
Jamesian pragmatism was democratic, individualistic,
humanistic, experimental, optimistic, and adventurous
in tone.[3] It can be quickly added that the same adjectives can be used to describe, as will be seen, the
reform spirit of Childs and his Progressive colleagues. In his typically spirited style, Childs captures
the essence of pragmatism's impact upon Progressive
reformism. He writes, "It was a time when the crust
of custom was being cracked. . . . *Change, invention,
novelty were in the air.*"[4]

Ralph Gabriel's caveat that "Progressivism was a

3. Henry Steele Commager, *The American Mind* (New Haven: Yale
University Press, 1950), pp. 95-96.
4. Richard S. Childs, ''The Coming of the Council-Manager Plan,''
February 21, 1963, p. 5 (mimeographed). (Italics mine.)

potpourri of theories and beliefs'"[5] is in order. There is, unfortunately, no concise definition of "Progressivism" within which Richard Childs may be placed. He and his era are too complex. However, there are certain basic aspects that deserve comment. If nothing else, the Progressive era, which covers roughly the first two decades of this century, was a period of dissent and revolt in America. This revolt cut through many phases of American intellectual life— literature, architecture, painting, religion, jurisprudence, sociology, economics, and last, but far from least, politics. Though an understanding of the general political milieu of the Progressive years is helpful for an insight into Childs's philosophy, of greatest value is an understanding of the urban political setting. This latter element is of such significance that it is treated separately in the succeeding section. In the present discussion of the impact of pragmatism and Progressivism upon Childs, it is sufficient to point out that the municipal reformer was revolting primarily against the city boss and his machine.

Childs in his reaction to machine politics believed, in the spirit of pragmatism, that "man," more specifically the "good government" advocates of which he was one, could manipulate the events, and this position, of course, was the more widely accepted one of the Progressive period. Childs charges, however, that Lincoln Steffens was a notable exception to this rule. Childs was greatly motivated by the moral ardor of *The Shame of the Cities*.[6] Yet, he claims that on the question of whether anything could be done about this "shame," he disagreed with Steffens.

5. Ralph H. Gabriel, *The Course of American Democratic Thought* (2d ed.; New York: Ronald Press Co., 1956), p. 360.
6. Interview with the author, January, 1964.

Taking strong issue with Steffens, Childs has written: "There was another prophet of doom, Lincoln Steffens! As a reporter of municipal corruption, superb, as diagnostician, all wet! For he sneeringly belittled our original Model Charter and our efforts to simplify the complex and preposterous mechanism of the democratic process, and took the line that, *whatever happened, the people were to blame.*"[7] This latter point is significant. Childs and his Progressive colleagues generally did not believe that "the people were to blame." Rather, it was the "politicians" and the governmental structure which favored the politicians" that were at fault.

As indicated, Commager contends that pragmatism was "optimistic" and "democratic" in mood.[8] These adjectives aptly describe Childs, and his brand of Progressive reformer, with their great confidence in "the people." With regard to the matter of "optimism," Woodrow Wilson, Childs's most famous associate in the short ballot movement, in *The New Freedom* clearly reveals this trait with this observation: "I believe, as I believe in nothing else in the average integrity and the average intelligence of the American people. . . . This great American people is at bottom just, virtuous, and hopeful. . . ."[9]

Throughout his book, *Short Ballot Principles*, written in 1909, Childs reveals strong faith in "the

7. Richard S. Childs, "Civic Victories in the United States," *National Municipal Review*, XXXXIV (September, 1955), 398. (Italics mine.) Chalmers writes of Steffens that "His primary concern was the bad citizenship of the American people and their failure to understand politics." David M. Chalmers, *The Social and Political Ideas of the Muckrakers* (New York: The Citadel Press, 1964), p. 77.

8. Commager, *The American Mind*, pp. 95-96.

9. Woodrow Wilson, *The New Freedom* (New York: Doubleday, Page and Co., 1913), pp. 64, 69.

American people," and he exudes "unclouded optimism."[10] As a result of this optimism in "the people,"
Progressive thought generally had unshakable confidence in the democratic process.[11] Throughout his
voluminous writings over the past half century, Childs
has adhered to this position. Repeatedly he has said
that "if it doesn't democ it isn't democracy!" In
1909, Childs wrote, "Democracy requires that the
people themselves get what they want, whether in
your opinion or mine it be altogether good for them
or not."[12] Consistently over the years he has held
faithfully to this tenet of Progressivism, even to the
extent of preferring "democracy" to "efficiency."
"Democracy," he contends, "is the prime objective,"
and not "money saving and greater efficiency. The
object is to make the democratic process genuinely
democratic. . . ."[13] Democracy was the supreme goal,
and the boss and his machine were antithetical to this
end. Childs captures the spirit of Progressive thought
with his observation, "So we political reformers are
always trying to get rid of such things as bosses and
machines by fixing up *the mechanism of democracy* to
work without such undemocratic interlopers."[14]

The key phrase is "the mechanism of democracy."

10. Richard S. Childs, *Short Ballot Principles* (Boston: Houghton
Mifflin Co., 1911), *passim*.
11. For general interpretations supporting this position, see Louis
Filler, *Crusaders for American Liberalism* (New York: Crowell-Collier
Publishing Co., 1961), p. 320, and Gabriel, *American Democratic
Thought*, p. 361.
12. Childs, *Short Ballot Principles*, p. 64.
13. Richard S. Childs, *The Charter Problem of Metropolitan Cities*
(New York: Citizens Union Research Foundation, Inc., 1960), p. 3, and
Childs, "The Coming of the Council-Manager Plan," p. 14. Also see
Richard S. Childs, *Civic Victories: The Story of an Unfinished Revolution* (New York: Harper and Brothers, 1952), pp. xvii, 8.
14. Richard S. Childs, "Ballot Is Still Too Long," *National Municipal Review*, XXXV (February, 1946), 67.

Lincoln Steffens notwithstanding, Childs and Progressive thinking generally believed that by tinkering with the mechanics of government its control could be taken from the boss and the machine and returned to "the people." The Progressive thinking developed a dichotomous view of the political struggle; it was a case of "the people" versus "the politician," and the mechanics of government had to be altered to restore the control of government to the former.[15] In 1909, Woodrow Wilson stated what was probably the basic tenet of mechanical reform. He explained, "Simplification—simplification—simplification is the task that awaits us."[16] Childs echoed the same sentiment in 1914 with his observation, "So, to make a long story short, the modern political scientist demands that politics shall be made primitively simple."[17]

This quest for simplicity brought a proliferation of ideas and mechanical concepts. In the words of Childs, "Political reform was boiling! . . . and assailing the . . . invisible governments with varied programs of reforms."[18] Certain fundamental notions of American government were attacked. It is significant that in this attack Childs and Progressivism stressed primarily the structural inadequacies of the American democratic system rather than any substantive shortcomings. Typical concepts attacked were what Childs called "ancient superstitions," i.e.,

15. For classic statements of this view, see Woodrow Wilson, "Hide-and-Seek Politics," *North American Review*, CXCI (May, 1910), 330-45, and Childs, "Politics Without Politicians," *The Saturday Evening Post*, pp. 5-6, 35.

16. Quoted in Childs, *Civic Victories*, p. 18.

17. Richard S. Childs, "County Manager Plan," *American City* (Town and Country Ed.), XI (December, 1914), 459.

18. Richard S. Childs, "Woodrow Wilson Legacy," *National Municipal Review*, XXXXVI (January, 1957), 14.

the doctrines of separation of power and checks and balances. Traditional American political thought accepted these principles, which insured weak government, as indispensable to democracy. Though surprisingly Childs had no particular quarrel with the structural scheme of the national government,[19] he strenuously argued, "that a miniature duplicate of the federal government was not the only conceivable basis for organization" of the other levels of government.[20] To insure mechanically perfect democracy Childs was in line with prevailing Progressive doctrine in contending for strong, unified, and integrated government. Childs unequivocally asserted, "The first job of reconstruction must be to integrate and unify the machinery of [local] government."[21] The theory was that with a mechanically "tight" governmental system—one that was simplified, unified, and integrated—democracy would inevitably ensue because the mechanism would be highly sensitive and responsive to the will of "the people." Childs concisely summed up this sentiment with his conclusion, "integration of powers of government is essential to effectiveness of popular control so that all the little packages come along when the voter lifts the string."[22] As shall be seen in the next chapter, the city manager concept of government is largely constructed on this premise.

19. In reference to the national government, Childs has written, "Its structure should be left alone—the founders of the republic got it pretty nearly right. . . ." Richard S. Childs, "Democracy That Might Work," *Century,* CXX (January, 1930), 16.

20. Childs, *Civic Victories,* p. 89.

21. Richard S. Childs, "How to Work for Charter Reform," *American City,* VIII (February, 1913), 150.

22. Childs, *Civic Victories,* p. 57.

Though the Progressive reformer, Childs included, rejected the doctrines of separation of powers and checks and balances as impediments in the quest of democracy, they eagerly accepted another form of "separation." This was the separation of politics and administration. As early as 1887, Woodrow Wilson in his classic article, "The Study of Administration," had propounded the idea of this dichotomy, and in the Progressive years that followed such well-known political scientists as Frank Goodnow and W. F. Willoughby continued to expound this "natural separation."[23] There is ample evidence that Childs has consistently over his lifetime adhered to this doctrinal tenet of Progressivism.[24] As Chapter III will reveal, this "principle" is fundamental in Childs's theory of city manager government.

"Simplification," "unification," "integration," rejection of the doctrine of separation of powers, and unswerving loyalty to the principle of the dichotomy of politics and administration were all prominent ideas in Progressive thought, and Richard S. Childs accepted them into his "arsenal" of municipal reform to re-establish local democracy.

However, beyond these basic and general areas of agreement, it is exceedingly difficult to find consensus in Progressivism. As mentioned, Commager states

23. Woodrow Wilson, "The Study of Administration," *Political Science Quarterly*, II (June, 1887), 197-222. Frank Goodnow, *Politics and Administration* (New York: The Macmillan Co., 1900). W. F. Willoughby, *The Government of Modern States* (New York: D. Appleton-Century Co., 1919).

24. For example, see Richard S. Childs, "Ramshackle County Government," *Outlook*, CXIII (May 3, 1916), 44; Committee Report, "Suggested Procedure for Selecting a City Manager," *National Municipal Review* (Supplement), XXII (December, 1933), 5; National Municipal League, *Model City Charter* (New York: National Municipal League, 1941); and, Childs, *Civic Victories*, p. 171.

that pragmatism, the philosophical foundation of Progressivism, was, among other things, "individualistic," "experimental," and "adventurous" in spirit. Because of these three characteristics, unanimity is nonexistent among Progressives as to the appropriate mechanical means to achieve democracy. Childs states the problem with his observation, "Progressivism blossomed out with programs,"[25] and he concludes, "Altogether a confusing time—the outstanding fact of the period being the avidity with which the public welcomed proposals for revising our institutions!"[26]

The "technical attack," as Childs called it, was off with a bang, and, as he notes further, each mechanical device offered to restore democracy was "sponsored by an eager group that frequently told the others that its reform was the only real one worthy of consideration."[27] First in point of time were the civil service reformers whose roots went back to the early years of the Gilded Age. As always, they contended they had the "true remedy," and that the outpouring of new mechanical prescriptions was unnecessary. However, the fervor of Progressivism swept over this faint protest. The air was charged with cries for the initiative, the referendum and recall, the preferential ballot, recall of judicial decisions, direct primaries, the commission plan of municipal government, proportional representation, bureaus of municipal research, and, Childs has reminisced, "In the midst of all this turmoil, I started shouting for

25. Richard S. Childs, "The League's Second Stretch," *National Municipal Review*, XXXIII (November, 1944), 514.

26. *Ibid.*, p. 515.

27. Richard S. Childs, "The City Manager Plan Will Endure," *American City*, LV (May, 1940), 35.

the short ballot idea and for its application in the municipal field in the form of a city manager plan.''[28] The short ballot movement merits extended discussion because of the central roles that Childs played in it, and it will be examined separately in a subsequent section of this chapter. The short ballot concept, coupled with its vehicle of transmission, the city manager form of government, represents, of course, Childs's major contribution to the municipal reform movement. Indeed, the manager form, discussed in detail in Chapter III, has become the principal municipal reform device of our time.

Childs concluded his book, *Short Ballot Principles,* with the exclamation that it was "a flag to follow." Then he asked his readers, "Are you with us!"[29] These small statements are illustrative of one basic and omnipresent attribute of Progressive reformism; namely, its zeal. Though the reformers might disagree on the appropriate mechanical device to achieve "true democracy," zeal is one constant element found in all of the reform programs of this era. Behind the façade of pragmatism, one finds a simple moralistic fervor. Zeal was not a new commodity in the reform tradition to be sure. The civil service reformers of the Gilded Age had displayed it; however, it rose to a fever pitch in the Progressive decades, and Childs reflects it. In his classic statement, titled "The Reformer," Childs writes, "[the reformer's] persistence against stone walls invites derision from those who have never been *touched by his religion and do not know what fun it is.*"[30] Repeatedly throughout

28. Richard S. Childs, "The New Opportunity for the City Manager Plan," *National Municipal Review,* XXII (January, 1933), 594.

29. Childs, *Short Ballot Principles,* pp. 170, 171.

30. Childs, *Civic Victories,* p. 338. (Italics mine.)

his writings Childs has emphasized "faith," "idealism," and "moral principles." His works are studded
with exclamation marks; as with many of his Progressive colleagues, his ardor never flags.

To this point I have attempted to show how Childs
shared certain basic tenets of the pragmatic and Progressive revolt. There are, however, areas in which
Childs "deviates" from Progressive political thought
generally. Significant, though perhaps not technically a deviation, is the fact that generally Childs has
confined his reform activity to the municipal level.[31]
There is no mystery involved. Basically this situation
has resulted as a matter of interest. Childs was first
and foremost concerned with "selling" the idea of the
short ballot. He believed that the national government
had, in effect, a short ballot because the electorate
voted only for four offices—the president and vice-
president, one senator, and a representative.[32] Thus
short ballot reform was simply inapplicable to the
national political structure. At the state and county
levels the crusade for short ballot reform has been
slow and grueling; at the local level, where the city
manager form of government has served as the device
for transmitting the short ballot, there has been, for
various reasons, an "impressive array of victories."
In short, the short ballot concept, plus the pattern of
success, has kept Childs laboring principally in the
field of municipal reform. In his preoccupation with
municipal reform, Childs presents no articulated
philosophy with respect to such significant Progressive ideals as Wilson's "New Freedom" or Croly's
"New Nationalism." As discussed, he shares their

31. For exceptions, see Chapter I.
32. Interview with the author, January, 1964.

general concern for integrated, positive, responsive, democratic government, but on balance Childs is not caught up in national Progressive politics of economic and social reform.[33]

Perhaps the most significant area of "deviation" relates to the inclination of Progressive thought to blame the business world, as well as the politicos, for the sad state of American politics. Hofstadter suggests that "big business was the ultimate enemy of the Progressive. . . ," while "his proximate enemy was the political machine."[34] Childs does not share this Progressive distrust of the business world nor its corollary of economic determinism seen in such eminent Progressive scholars as Beard and Veblen.[35] When asked if he had agreed with Upton Sinclair's and Lincoln Steffens' proposals for public ownership of municipal utilities, Childs replied, "No. After all, I was the son of a capitalist."[36]

The place of William Hamlin Childs, Richard's father, in the development of his son's thinking is

33. Robert H. Wiebe concludes, "The only important contribution which businessmen made to the social welfare movement came as a by-product of their zeal for civic improvement. As they scrubbed and polished their cities, some of them did assist in improving local housing and health codes." *Businessmen and Reform* (Cambridge: Harvard University Press, 1962), p. 212. For evidence that Childs had a broader vision of municipal reform than the businessmen Wiebe describes, see the final section of the concluding chapter.

Wiebe's study is the most comprehensive one concerning the role of businessmen in the national Progressive movement.

34. Richard Hofstadter, *The Age of Reform: From Bryan to F. D. R.* (New York: Vintage Books, Inc., 1960), p. 257. Also see Chalmers, *Muckrakers*, pp. 106-107.

35. The only solid evidence where Childs suggests culpability on the part of the business groups is his assertion in 1909 that "ramshackle government" could not be expected to stand up to the pressures of the big private corporations; hence he argued for strong, unified, and integrated government. See Childs, *Short Ballot Principles*, p. 128.

36. Interview with the author, January, 1964.

extensively analyzed in the following section. It is sufficient here to note that he was a highly successful businessman who, in addition to participating actively in Progressive Party politics, had labored for political and civic reform in his native New York City.[37] As the succeeding section discloses, his opposition to Tammany Hall had culminated in the unjustified indictment brought against him following the bitter mayoralty campaign of 1917. His son had seen responsible capitalism first hand,[38] and in Tammany he had been an eyewitness to the evils of the urban machine. Perhaps it is not surprising, therefore, that he did not share that segment of Progressive thought which held the business community primarily responsible for the sordid state of affairs in America's great cities. He placed the blame squarely upon the politicos, and throughout his long career he has considered them the "number one" enemy. All efforts, all exhortations have been directed to the task of expelling them from the municipal political scene. As Childs has summed it up, "So our goal is democracy in a truly workable form, free of such oddities as bossism, rings, or tight self-renewing cliques of politicians, regardless of whether taxes go up or down!"[39]

37. Illustrative of his civic consciousness was his donation of $250,000 to the Bowling Green Neighborhood for "the perpetual welfare of the men, women and children who live and work in lower Manhattan." *New York Times*, January 26, 1925, p. 1, col. 4. At his funeral in 1928 the Reverend John Barlow eulogized, "He loved to not only be good, but to do good. He aimed to not only get something out of life, but to put something in it. He succeeded in both." *Ibid.*, November 6, 1928, p. 27, col. 4.

38. William Hamlin Childs may be an exception to Wiebe's conclusion that "Progressive businessmen singularly lacked a grand social vision. Placing reform on a business basis, they represented . . . the hard side of progressivism." Wiebe, *Businessmen and Reform*, p. 217.

39. Childs, *Civic Victories*, p. xvii.

Urbanism and Machine Politics

The period following the Civil War and leading to the turn of the century produced drastic changes in the American scene. The rise of heavy industry during the Gilded Age introduced a fantastic new stage in industrial growth. Inseparable from this development was the urban "explosion" and the immigrant flood that poured in from Europe. As Commager states it, the decade of the 1890's was the "watershed" of American history.[40] America was transformed from an agricultural nation to an industrial, urbanized one. It is this process of urbanization, and the ultimate political ramifications, that explains much about Richard Childs.

Into the burgeoning urban community with its increased influx of immigrant labor[41] came that political institution, "the machine." To an America of a more simple and genteel past, the increasing growth and perfection of the machine was a shocking development; it represented the prostitution of the democratic process, for in return for the votes of the poor confused immigrant the machine returned a *quid pro quo* of personal "services." These services might range from supplying a turkey for Christmas to the greatest of all—providing employment. As Edward J. Flynn, who was certainly in a position to know, cogently put

40. Commager, *The American Mind,* Chapter II, "The Watershed of the Nineties."
41. Hofstadter records that the "steady stream of immigrants . . . reached its peak in 1907 when 1,285,000 immigrant entries were recorded. By 1910, 13,345,000 foreign-born persons were living in the United States, or almost one seventh of the total population." Hofstadter, *The Age of Reform,* p. 177. It is significant that in these years at this crest of the immigrant tide that Childs was embarking upon his career of municipal reform.

it, "Ninety-nine out of a hundred [immigrants] want jobs first and political theorizing afterward."[42]

The machine, however, had its less appealing side. Bribery, corruption of police, graft, rampant prostitution, and poor municipal services, coupled with high taxes, were often the rule. By the 1890's Lord Bryce could contend that the government of American cities was "the one conspicuous failure of the United States,"[43] and Andrew D. White could assert that "with very few exceptions, the city governments of the United States are the worst in Christendom—the most expensive, the most inefficient, and the most corrupt."[44] As recent scholars have observed, "The reformers had reason to be shocked by the facts of urban life."[45]

The reform spirit grew with increasing strength in reaction to these conditions. The first great milestone was passed with the founding of the National Municipal League in 1894—Richard Childs was twelve at this time. The Municipal League of Philadelphia and the City Club of New York City, the latter composed of such eminent first-generation municipal reformers as Charles Francis Adams, Carl Schurz, William Dudley Foulke, and Dorman B. Eaton, had jointly called for "A National Conference for Good City Government." The result was the formation of the National Municipal League, and the battle for municipal reform was on. In the words of Clifford W.

42. Edward J. Flynn, *You're the Boss* (New York: The Viking Press, 1947), p. 25.

43. James Bryce, *The American Commonwealth* (New York: The Macmillan Co., 1897), I, 637.

44. Andrew D. White, *Forum*, X (December, 1890), 25.

45. Gladys M. Kammerer, Charles D. Farris, John M. DeGrove, and Alfred B. Clubok, *The Urban Political Community* (Boston: Houghton Mifflin Co., 1963), p. 1.

Patton, this ferment "evolved into the clearer voice of a new century."[46]

One of these clearer voices was that of Lincoln Steffens, who, Regier states, is in some respects the "real founder of the muckraking movement."[47] *The Shame of the Cities* appeared in 1904, the same year that Richard Childs, a young man of twenty-two, graduated from Yale. As noted, Childs considers this book as having had a conscious impact upon his thinking.[48] Steffens exposed the miasma that existed in America's machine-governed cities—in St. Louis, Minneapolis, Chicago, Philadelphia, Pittsburgh, and New York City, and he confirmed what Childs had been learning firsthand in New York. The latter point warrants emphasis.

Pragmatism, Progressivism, and the industrial-urban revolution generally were all a part of the milieu of the young Childs and conditioned his thinking; however, the fact that he has lived in New York City nearly all of his life, and has sensed, seen, and participated in the politics of America's largest city, has influenced him incalculably. The impact of the "Tammany Tiger" cannot be passed over lightly.

46. Clifford W. Patton, *The Battle for Municipal Reform* (Washington, D.C.: American Council on Public Affairs, 1940), p. 76.

47. C. C. Regier, *The Era of the Muckrakers* (Chapel Hill: University of North Carolina Press, 1932), p. 59.

48. Interview with the author, January 7, 1964. Childs also emphasized in an interview the impact of Henry George and his *Progress and Poverty* upon his thinking. Childs stated he was impressed with the idea of a single tax, though he rejected any form of doctrinal socialism. Probably it was George's fervent reaction to the evils of urban industrialism that most impressed Childs, rather than the specific remedy. Although Childs was only four years of age in 1886 when George first ran for Mayor of New York City, both men were eye witnesses to the industrial-urban revolution in that city, and, in the spirit of American pragmatism, both believed that "man" could do something to correct its pernicious effects.

Childs traces his insatiable interest in municipal reform to a single evening in 1897 when, as a lad of fifteen, he was taken by his father to a political rally being held on behalf of Seth Low, former reform mayor of Brooklyn and President of Columbia University, who was running as the first reform mayor of a consolidated New York City. Childs relates that at this rally there was "electricity in the air," and the issue was drawn between the forces of "good" versus the forces of "evil." Tammany Hall was the force of evil, of course, and a famed political cartoon of the day, in reference to the consolidation, depicted the Tammany Tiger crossing the Brooklyn Bridge. At this rally, Childs claims, his passion for reform was born.[49]

It was, therefore, his father who introduced Richard to the glories—and disappointments—of the struggle for municipal reform. The founder of the Bon Ami Company, William Hamlin Childs was a highly successful businessman,[50] and active in political and civic causes in New York City. An ardent supporter of Theodore Roosevelt in the presidential election of 1912 and an uncompromising backer of "T. R." for the presidency in 1916 before the eventual nomination of Charles Evans Hughes, he served as Chairman of the Kings County Progressive Committee.[51] It was in 1917 that he had his most strenuous political encounter, and that occurred at home in New York City.

49. Interview with the author, January, 1964.
50. He died in 1928 and left a net estate, valued in 1930 at nearly six million dollars, to his wife and two children, Richard and Mary. At the time of his death he was chairman of the board of the Bon Ami Company, which he had founded, and a director in many other corporations. *New York Times*, November 22, 1930, p. 17, col. 3.
51. *Ibid.*, November 3, 1928, p. 19, col. 3; May 8, 1916, p. 5, col. 2; June 29, 1916, p. 22, col. 3.

The municipal election of 1917 was bitterly fought between the reform mayor John Purroy Mitchel, the "Fusion" ticket candidate, and John F. Hylan, Tammany Hall's choice. William Childs was in the thick of the fight as Chairman of the Fusion Executive Committee[52] and Chairman of Mitchel's campaign committee. Mayor Mitchel argued that the dominant issue "was, of course, Murphyism [Charles F. Murphy was the Tammany boss] and Tammany Hall,"[53] while William Childs pleaded for "a continuance of this clean, honest, businesslike program."[54] However, the Tammany machine of Charles Murphy prevailed, and the reform administration of John Mitchel came to an abrupt end.[55]

Unsatisfied with victory at the polls, the Tammany machine began criminal proceedings against William Childs on a patently technical and unwarranted charge of violating the election laws regarding financial reports. An indictment was returned against him on April 17, 1914,[56] and he charged that the whole affair was an "outrageous political attack."[57] Richard Childs was incensed with the Tammany machinations. He wrote, "What a reward for so valiant and brilliant an effort! I was sick about it. It was a purely political thrust."[58] It was not until four long years later,

52. The Fusion Party was composed of Republicans, independents, and Democrats disenchanted with the Tammany-Hall wing of their party.

53. *New York Times*, October 18, 1917, p. 3, col. 5.

54. *Ibid.*, June 25, 1917, p. 10, col. 8.

55. For a favorable account of the Mitchel administration, see Gustavus Myers, *The History of Tammany Hall* (New York: Boni and Liveright, Inc., 1917), pp. 399-403.

56. *New York Times*, April 17, 1918, p. 24, col. 2.

57. *Ibid.*, September 16, 1918, p. 13, col. 3.

58. Richard S. Childs, *William Hamlin Childs* (privately printed, 1957), p. 22.

after many legal entanglements, that Tammany ultimately called off the prosecution and the indictment was dismissed.[59] Childs asserted this ugly affair further confirmed what he had learned at the rally for Seth Low in 1897—that machine politics was evil, particularly the Tammany brand, and that, though he was already laboring hard for municipal reform, more must be done; the fight must never cease! Childs's residency in New York City has continually influenced his philosophy and has kept his reform fervor at a high pitch.[60]

Specific Elements of Childs's Philosophy

Scientific Management

Childs states that he has not read the works of Frederick W. Taylor nor, to his knowledge, have Taylor's ideas had a conscious impact upon his thinking.[61] Probably the important word here is "conscious." Problems of causation in the social sciences are complex; nevertheless, when an individual strongly reflects a major philosophical trend of his milieu, though admittedly precise indices of "scientific" measurement are conspicuously absent, we are probably reasonable in concluding that the philosophy in question has had an impact, consciously or unconsciously. This premise applies to Richard Childs in the case of pragmatism, Progressivism, scientific management, and the other intellectual currents subsequently discussed in this chapter.

At many points of contact Progressivism and

59. *New York Times*, January 1, 1922, p. 9, col. 5.
60. For a discussion of Childs's political activities in New York City in the decades following the Progressive era, see Chapter I.
61. Interview with the author, January, 1964.

scientific management are inseparable. In point of time the scientific management school rose to acclaim contemporaneously with the reform movement. Though its roots go back into the Gilded Age, this movement reached its peak under the leadership of Frederick W. Taylor after 1911 with his publication of *The Principles of Scientific Management.*[62] Significantly, this school was reaching its zenith of popularity at the time Richard Childs was commencing his career of selling the ideas of the short ballot and city manager government.

Progressive thought heartily embraced the "scientific" spirit. Concomitant with this spirit arose the penchant in business and public administration for efficiency and *expertise*. This Progressive quest for efficiency per se[63] and *expertise* centered in the disciples of Taylor.

In theory scientific management was empirical in approach for it stressed "scientific" method and the accumulation of facts. From these "facts," as the following section of this chapter will suggest, were developed incontrovertible "principles." The development of a "principle," in substance, meant the discovery of a "one-best way" to accomplish any given task, which in turn produced the ultimate value of efficiency. As a corollary to this achievement of efficiency, was the search for the expert and his *expertise*. This effort was more commonly known as the quest for the "one-best man."

Though Taylorism was initially conceived as applicable only to industry and commerce, it soon spread into the field of public administration and was

62. (New York: Harper and Brothers, 1911.)
63. Efficiency per se as a goal meant, fundamentally, maximum output with a minimum input; however, it did not mean niggardliness.

reflected strongly in the academic thinking of that area. Richard S. Childs is an excellent illustration. To begin with, the entire concept of the council-manager plan is patterned after a business model of organization. As Chapter III indicates, Childs patterned the manager form on that of the private business corporation. The city council is analogous to the corporate board of directors, while the city manager is comparable to the corporate president. The rationale in large part is that since the private corporation is managed so efficiently with this organizational form, no reason exists why it should not be applied to a "business" owned and operated by the public.[64]

Chapter III discloses in depth that, in keeping with the spirit of scientific management, Childs in effect constructs a "machine model" of municipal government. A desirable goal is a "smooth-running [or efficient] mechanism," as the following comment by Childs in 1913 clearly demonstrates. He wrote, "It is easily possible to contrive a representative *mechanism which will automatically produce* whatever kind of government the people want. . . . The mechanism . . . can be made extremely sensitive to public control. . . ."[65] At a later date Childs confirmed this observation with the conclusion, "Weak, ramshackle governmental organizations are not merely *inherently inefficient* but have the cranky disobedience of faulty ill-designed mechanisms. . . ."[66]

64. For the earliest statement by Childs employing this reasoning, see Richard S. Childs, "Lockport Proposal to Improve the Commission Plan," *American City*, IV (June, 1911), 286.
65. Richard S. Childs, "How to Work for Charter Reform," *American City*, VIII (February, 1913), 149. (Italics mine.)
66. Richard S. Childs, "Democracy That Might Work," *Century*, CXX (January, 1930), 15. (Italics mine.)

In further keeping with Taylorism, Childs—consciously or unconsciously—accepts the idea of discovering a "one-best way." Childs considers his "brain child," the city-manager form, as the one-best way to govern the cities of America. Illustrative is his comment, "So we may reasonably hope that these . . . years may be seen by future historians as the ones in which America *found the correct form* of city government and proved its correctness. . . ."[67]

The Taylorist theory of the discovery—through "scientific" method—of the "one-best man" is also reflected in Childs's philosophy of municipal government. Throughout his writings there is ample evidence to indicate that he visualizes the selection of the individual candidates for the council as a task of comparing the various competing candidates on a man-to-man basis, and then selecting the one-best candidate.[68] Furthermore, the selection of the city manager, as envisaged by Childs, is patently an application of the "one-best-man" approach. There is "an ideal way to go about it,"[69] and in the words of the National Municipal League Committee on which Childs served, "If the difficult task of selecting a properly qualified manager is *faithfully carried out,* an efficient and economical administration is practically assured"[70] because the one-best manager will inevitably be chosen.[71]

67. Richard S. Childs, "Rise and Spread of the City Manager Plan of Local Government," *American City,* XXXXIII (September, 1930), 131. (Italics mine.)

68. For early evidence of this approach, see Childs, *Short Ballot Principles,* p. 136.

69. Committee Report, "Selecting a City Manager," *National Municipal Review* (Supplement).

70. *Ibid.,* p. 3. (Italics mine.)

71. In 1927, Leonard D. White happily reported, "Many councils have gone about the search for the 'one-best man' with a deliberation

In suggesting these striking similarities between Childs's political thought and the scientific management movement, a caveat, already alluded to in this chapter, is in order. Though Childs repeatedly supports the Taylorist concept of "efficiency," if he must choose between efficiency, and that other strong doctrinal tenet of Progressivism, "democracy," he will opt for the latter because "democracy is the prime objective."[72] Consistently throughout his career Childs has held to this position; yet, in the final analysis, he sees no reason why such a cruel dilemma —the choice between democracy and efficiency—need arise. Progressive thought—and Childs is no exception—classified democracy and efficiency as compatible elements. Typical is Childs's conclusion, "And as the further fruit of the election of able, public spirited, nonpolitical councils, it is demonstrated that *efficiency is reconcilable with American democracy!*"[73]

The "Principles Approach"

Though this approach is an integral part of the scientific management school, and inseparable from it, there is, however, heuristic value in introducing this additional category in understanding Childs's philosophy.

For centuries political philosophers had been expounding the "higher-law" concepts or principles of the natural law, and, indeed, since Hobbes there had been an empirical bent to the pursuit of these uni-

and care worthy of the highest commendation." *The City Manager* (Chicago: University of Chicago Press, 1927), p. 172.

72. See references in footnote 13, p. 20.

73. Childs, *Civic Victories*, p. 188. (Italics mine.)

versal and immutable principles by which men governed themselves. However, it was in the late nineteenth and early twentieth centuries in America when the worship of "science" produced the claim that incontestable principles governing human affairs might be discovered by appropriate scientific method. As noted in the preceding section, the scientific management movement gave credence to this claim. It stressed scientific method, accumulation of the "facts," and from this the construction of immutable laws or principles of universal application. These doctrinal tenets of Taylorism, developed for industrial production, were before long applied to business administration and then to the study of public administration.

In 1919, W. F. Willoughby wrote, "There are certain fundamental principles and practices which must obtain in all governmental undertakings, if efficiency and economy in operation are to be secured."[74] Classic is the assertion by Lyndall Urwick that, "There are certain principles which govern the association of human beings *for any purpose,* just as there are certain engineering principles which govern the building of a bridge."[75] Many students of American politics were caught up in this search for "principles" of government, and Richard Childs was among them.

The concept of the short ballot principle, discussed in the final section of this chapter, is essentially based

74. G. A. Weber, *Organized Efforts for the Improvement of Methods of Administration in the United States* (New York: Brookings Institute, 1919), p. 30.

75. Lyndall Urwick, "Executive Decentralization with Functional Coordination," *Public Administration Review,* XIII (Spring, 1935), 344. (Italics mine.)

upon the "principles approach." Specifically, through the accumulation of "facts," an incontestable "principle" of democratic government is established.[76] Childs's other mechanism of reform, the council-manager plan, is similarly based. As Chapter III discloses, Childs constructs his machine model of municipal government upon a foundation of "sound principles," after having rejected the mayoralty and commission forms as violative of these same rules.[77] These "principles" are considered immutable and of universal application. Childs is unequivocal in this regard: "In small cities and large, the period of practical testing is completed. The plan is no longer to be regarded merely as an interesting and sensible looking novelty but as a well-proven fixture destined to become the prevailing form of a municipal government in America. *It only remains* to extend the plan to the remaining two thousand cities and to perfect ways to apply *the same basic principles to state and county governments.*"[78]

The "Organizational-Chart Approach"

This approach is closely allied to the "principles approach." In the latter case it is contended that the

76. The method by which "facts" are accumulated is not spelled out by any proponents of the approach and, therefore, is not susceptible to replication. As a consequence, the definition of "fact" is not faced.

77. For early evidence of Childs's having reduced the matter of council-manager government to a set of principles, see Richard S. Childs, "The Principles Underlying the Plan," in *Commission Government with a City Manager* (New York: The National Short Ballot Organization, 1914), pp. 12-22.

78. Richard S. Childs, "Along the Governmental Battle Front," *National Municipal Review*, XIX (January, 1930), 5. (Italics mine.) For earlier evidence showing that Childs held this attitude, see Richard S. Childs, *The Story of the Short Ballot Cities* (New York: The National Short Ballot Organization, 1914), p. 18.

problems of administration can be reduced to a set of discoverable "scientific principles," and in the "organizational-chart approach" the theory is offered that the formal organization—the crux of organizational problems—should be constructed upon the applicable principles. Lyndall Urwick is an excellent example of the combined impact of these two approaches on the study of American public administration. He has written, "The idea that organization should be built up around and adjusted to individual idiosyncrasies, rather than that individuals should be adapted to the requirements of *sound principles of organization*, is . . . foolish. . . ."[79] Mooney in his article in the classic *Papers on the Science of Administration* concisely stated the sentiments of the organizational-chart school with the observation, "Ten to one we must go to organization rather than personnel to find the real cause of trouble."[80]

In the earlier section on "Pragmatism and Progressivism," it was brought out that Progressive reformers, including Richard Childs, stressed the use of mechanical devices to correct the ills besetting the democratic process. The emphasis in the field of public administration on the formal organizational structure reflected a similar mood with regard to the problems of the administrative process.

Woodrow Wilson, one of the towering figures of Progressivism, manifested this preoccupation in public administration with the formal elements of organization, and, in particular, he found the problems of

79. Lyndall Urwick, "Organization as a Technical Problem," in Luther Gulick and Lyndall Urwick (eds.), *Papers on the Science of Administration* (New York: Institute of Public Administration, 1937), p. 85. (Italics mine.)

80. James D. Mooney, "The Principles of Organization," in *ibid.*, p. 92.

municipal government basically organizational ones. In 1910 he offered this explanation for the evils of local government: "Most of the badly governed cities of the civilized world are on this side of the Atlantic, most of the well governed on the other side; and the reason is not accidental. It has nothing to do with principle or of national character. It results from *differences of organization of the most fundamental and important kind which cut to the very roots of the whole matter.*"[81]

Richard Childs has taken the same tack. For example, the concepts of the short ballot and the city and county manager forms of government are predicated upon the belief that the difference in organizational structure is *the* single causal difference between "good" and "bad" government. With his ever present disdain for "the politicians," Childs argues that they have flourished because the organizational form of government—or "battleground" as he calls it—has been "rigged" in their favor; the result has been "bad" government, and he proposes to change all of this through an alteration in the structure of government.

An excellent illustration of this approach is Childs's analysis of the problem of "ramshackle county government" in America. The county form of government Childs heartily detests because it is "the uttermost citadel of our political overlords."[82] According to his analysis, that citadel can be destroyed in only one way: change the structure. He has concluded: "The diagram of a typical county, when all the inter-relations [*sic*] of the various officials are

81. Wilson, "Hide-and-Seek Politics," *North American Review*, p. 597. (Italics mine.)
82. Childs, "Ramshackle County Government," *Outlook*, p. 45.

represented by lines, looks like a ball of yarn after the cat has gotten through with it. . . . Political science, however, sees in pulling and hauling, deadlocks and delays, merely the symptom of a disease, and, disregarding all the immediate factors, *seeks a form of organization* for the county. . . . *The political scientist proceeds to lay the blame once again on the kind of organization.*"[83] With the penchant for mechanical metaphors common during the heyday of Progressivism and scientific management, Childs further comments, "In its form of organization the typical county is ideally bad. . . . It is like an auto with a separate motor at every wheel, each going its own gait."[84] In essence there is one variable that holds the key to reform—the properly charted formal organization.

The Short Ballot Movement

Strictly speaking, of course, the short ballot movement is not a "foundation" of Childs's philosophy as its inclusion in this chapter might suggest. More accurately it is a manifestation of the "foundations" discussed in the previous sections, and for this reason is included at this point.

Sharing Progressive hostility for the politicos, Childs organized this movement practically single-handedly in a crusading effort to thwart the spoilsmen. Childs has related how he reacted in 1903 at the tender age of twenty-one to his first voting experi-

83. Childs, ''County Manager Plan,'' *American City*, p. 457. (Italics mine.)
84. Childs, ''Ramshackle County Government,'' *Outlook*, p. 43.

ence: "I entered a polling booth and unfolded my first ballot. I found to my dismay that I was hopelessly unprepared. There near the top were the four principal candidates . . . but there were fifteen other officers to be elected. . . . On these latter . . . I had no information. . . . With mortification I voted blindly for the word 'Republican' in each of the fifteen contests and thereby, of course, accepted without scrutiny the offerings of the party leaders, as they knew I would."[85] Young Childs decided, "The long ballot is the politician's ballot; the short ballot is the people's ballot!"[86] In the true spirit of pragmatism—through the "efficacy of effort"—Childs resolved to do something about it.

A major breakthrough came in 1909 with the publication in *Outlook* magazine of his article, "The Short Ballot." This was his first venture in publication, and it proved highly successful. As compared with European cities, their American counterparts were characterized by Childs in this way: "Good administration is actually abnormal. . . . Maladministration is the normal."[87] Clearly influenced by the assumption that there must be a mechanical or formal organizational defect, he continued, "This condition . . . indicates the existence of some peculiarity in our system of government as *the* underlying cause."[88] This "underlying cause" or variable is the long ballot —the "politician's ballot," and Childs's remedy is to alter the structure to conform with "sound princi-

85. Childs, *Civic Victories*, p. 22.
86. *Ibid.*, p. 11.
87. Richard S. Childs, "The Short Ballot," *Outlook*, LXXXII (July, 1909), 635.
88. *Ibid.*, p. 635. (Italics mine.)

ples"—in this case the "short ballot principles."[89] Childs made it clear in this classic article that there is a single-cause explanation for the ills affecting municipal government in the United States. Displaying Progressive zeal for the recovery of "democracy," he concluded, "And we can win back our final freedom on a 'short ballot' basis!"[90] This position was similar to the cry of the earlier civil service reformers who attributed the ills of government to a single cause: the spoils system.

In 1908, one year before he got his idea into print, Childs brought into operation his considerable organizational talents. He privately circulated copies of his article among distinguished reformers of the day to test their interest in supporting an organization to propagate the short ballot principle. He also took the article to some of his old Yale professors who responded that the concept was "both new and true."[91] The first gentleman to answer to his program of private circulation of the article was Sir James Bryce, author of *The American Commonwealth* (which Childs some years before had avidly read),[92] and at the time British ambassador to the United States. Bryce enjoyed great vogue among American municipal reformers, and it was he who had said that America's

89. The National Short Ballot Organization stated in its materials: "The 'SHORT BALLOT' principle is: First—that only those offices should be elective which are important enough to attract (and deserve) public examination. Second—that very few offices should be filled by election at one time, so as to permit adequate and unconfused public examination of the candidates. Obedience to these fundamental principles explains [successful democratic government in certain areas of the world]. The application of these principles should be extended to all cities, counties and states." Childs, *The Story of the Short Ballot Cities*, p. 18.

90. Childs, "The Short Ballot," *Outlook*, p. 635.

91. Childs, "The Coming of the Council-Manager Plan," p. 5.

92. Interview with the author, January, 1964.

cities were its "one conspicuous failure." He wrote an enthusiastic letter to Childs and concluded, "I hope you will continue to write along these lines."[93] Childs was elated and exclaimed, "This was praise from Caesar!"[94]

He received many encouraging replies, and his task then became that of selecting those whom he would ask to lend the prestige of their names to the organization's letterhead. Childs frankly admits he avoided certain famous personages on the theory that they were too "radical"; they would bring more controversy than assistance. One such person was William Jennings Bryan, who did support the short ballot principle.[95] Though some historians might consider the Populist as the ancestor of the Progressive, the latter, if a municipal reformer, by no means always regarded his rural counterpart in that way, and Childs's avoidance of "radical" support was probably in keeping with a not uncommon Progressive attitude.

By no means, however, did Childs attempt to make his short ballot movement strictly one of "silk-stocking" or elite urban Progressivism. For example, in the initial organization of the National Short Ballot Organization in 1909, Childs selected as one of the vice-presidents the controversial social reformer and juvenile judge from Denver, Judge Ben B. Lindsey. Even though Childs had never personally met Lindsey, he selected him for the esteem his name would lend to the newborn organization. Furthermore, in 1912, Childs chose the famous union leader of the mine workers, John Mitchell, as one of the honorary

93. *Ibid.*
94. *Ibid.*
95. *The Short Ballot Bulletin* (New York: The National Short Ballot Organization, 1911-1920), VII, p. 4.

vice-presidents, to emphasize the "catholic character of our movement."[96]

Although Childs had not met him, the famous Kansan William Allen White consented to serve as an honorary vice-president in the original organization, and he often supported the short ballot principle with editorials. Winston Churchill, the popular Progressive novelist, also lent the prestige of his name as a vice-president, as did the noted Oregon reformer and expounder of the initiative, referendum, and recall, William U'ren. Childs was anxious to have U'ren's support, for this in turn would assure western reform support generally.[97] To complete his list of vice-presidents Childs chose Horace E. Deming, a political scientist and active figure in the National Municipal League, and Clinton Rodgers Woodruff, a lawyer from Philadelphia, and also an avid supporter of the National Municipal League, who had participated in the 1894 convention that established that organization.

To serve on his "advisory board" for the National Short Ballot Organization, Childs secured an equally imposing group of volunteers. Lawrence F. Abbott, son of the famous Lyman Abbott and close friend of William Hamlin Childs, agreed to serve. He was editor of *Outlook* magazine, the periodical in which Richard Childs's classic little article, "The Short Ballot," had appeared. Also serving were the dis-

96. *Ibid.*, I, 1.
97. Interview with the author, January, 1964. Childs in a letter dated October 22, 1963, wrote, "U'ren came east in those years; and when we met, he said that if he had learned of the short ballot principle earlier, he would have given his efforts to it rather than to the work for which he acquired fame. . . ." Letter to the author, October 22, 1963.

tinguished Princeton professor Henry Jones Ford and Norman Hapgood, the crusading editor of *Collier's Weekly*. In addition to his occupancy of a position on the advisory board, Childs served as secretary and treasurer of the fledgling organization, while H. S. Gilbertson, a graduate student at Columbia University recommended to Childs by Charles A. Beard, served as executive secretary.

The prize "catch" by Childs, of course, was Woodrow Wilson, twenty-six years his senior and President of Princeton University, who consented to serve as president of the organization and as a member of the advisory board. It was through the help of Arthur C. Ludington, a preceptor at Princeton under the presidency of Wilson whom Childs met through the City Club in New York City, that the introduction to the Princeton president was arranged for Childs. Wilson was genuinely enthusiastic over Child's short ballot principle.[98] With characteristic Progressive zeal for a return to "true democracy," Wilson exclaimed in a 1909 speech, "I believe that the short ballot is *the key* to the whole question of the restoration of government by the people."[99] During the following year he stated, "This process of simplification [by means of the short ballot] is our *only salvation.*"[100] With this kind of unstinting praise it is not surprising that Childs should relate,

98. Arthur S. Link writes that the short ballot principle "became almost an obsession" with Wilson. See *Wilson: The Road to the White House* (Princeton, N.J.: Princeton University Press, 1947), p. 125. Childs denies that there was any obsession and insists that Wilson was quite "logical and reasonable" about the matter. Interview with the author, January, 1964.
99. Quoted in Link, *Wilson*, p. 124. (Italics mine.)
100. Quoted in *ibid*. (Italics mine.)

"We readily combined doctrines and zeal in founding the Short Ballot Organization."[101]

To finance his newly founded organization, Childs was fortunate in having a wealthy as well as civic-minded father. Though slightly skeptical at the outset as to whether the short ballot principle was *the* solution, as his enthusiastic son contended that it was, William Childs's doubts were allayed by Woodrow Wilson and Henry Jones Ford.[102] The elder Childs, therefore, provided ten thousand dollars a year for operating expenses.[103] All considered, the new venture was off to an auspicious start.

In 1911, Childs's first book, *Short Ballot Principles*, was published. Exuding Progressive enthusiasm for "democracy," disdain of the "politician" and his machine, and predilection for *the* appropriate mechanical device to return control of the government to "the people," Childs, in commenting on many structural features of the American political scene,[104] basically offered the short ballot concept as "the flag to follow."

Childs related that it was Charles A. Beard who proposed the basic format of presentation of *Short*

101. Richard S. Childs, "Half Century of Municipal Reform," *American Journal of Economics and Sociology*, XV (April, 1956), 322.

102. Interview with the author, January, 1964.

103. Childs, *William Hamlin Childs*, p. 20.

104. Gilbertson, on behalf of the National Short Ballot Organization, found it necessary to disclaim that Wilson had had anything to do with the writing of the book because "some of the suggestions are novel and radical," and they became a slight cloud on Wilson's candidacy for the presidency. To eliminate the embarrassment to Wilson from the "novel and radical" ideas, Gilbertson wrote, "Any attempt therefore to credit the Governor with desire to abolish counties for example, or to reconstruct political parties on new lines is far-fetched and unfair." The Childs Papers on the National Short Ballot Organization, Vol. II, p. 42.

Ballot Principles.[105] Both men lived in New York City. Beard was at Columbia University then, and, as a consequence, they had opportunities for face-to-face encounters. Although Beard explicitly endorsed the short ballot concept,[106] he would not permit his name to be used on the letterhead of the National Short Ballot Organization. Beard was suspect of any a priori ideal system,[107] and, as Childs put it, he was eager to "protect that image."[108] Therefore, he declined to endorse the short ballot principle publicly by permitting his name to be listed as an officer of the organization. In short, Beard was a faithful pragmatist in the tradition of William James because he rarely found (and endorsed) "truth" with a capital *T*.[109]

For a period of nine years, from 1911 to 1920, the Short Ballot Organization published at frequent intervals *The Short Ballot Bulletin,* which in effect was a leaflet giving a progress report on the successes of the movement. Childs was, of course, the guiding hand in its publication. The *Bulletins* in the early years supported the commission form of government as the appropriate instrument for instituting short ballot principles; however, as Childs nurtured the city manager concept into a weapon of reform, the *Bulletins*

105. Interview with the author, January, 1964.
106. Charles A. Beard, ''The Ballot's Burden,'' *Political Science Quarterly,* XXIV (December, 1909), 589-614.
107. Dwight Waldo, *The Administrative State* (New York: Ronald Press Co., 1948), p. 84.
108. Interview with the author, January, 1964.
109. Childs states that for many years Beard withheld approval of the council-manager form of government, and when he did extend his blessing, he withheld it in the case of the larger cities. Interview with the author, January, 1964. Furthermore, Beard was outspoken in his criticism of the nonpartisan dimension of the reform movement. In 1917 he wrote, ''I am prepared to defend the thesis that nonpartisanship has not worked, does not work, and will not work in any major city in the United States.'' Charles A. Beard, ''Politics and City Government,'' *National Municipal Review,* VI (March, 1917), 205.

gradually, and with gusto after adoption of the new form of government by Sumter, came around to the manager plan as the proper device for carrying short ballot doctrine to America's cities. *The Short Ballot Bulletin* ceased to be published when the National Short Ballot Organization merged with the National Municipal League in 1920. Childs shifted his energies to the League after the merger.

The short ballot movement bears witness to the extraordinary organizational talents of Richard Childs. If it is ever possible for one man to bring an organization to life, Childs did so with this movement. He formulated the idea, personally solicited the backing of his distinguished supporters, and carried the organization through to remarkable successes. Wilson, as the most distinguished figure in it, exercised the final veto on a few minor points and reserved the right to approve the names of those who were listed on the letterhead along with him.[110] Beyond this authority, Childs has stated that Wilson "trusted him implicitly" and never admonished or corrected him on any matter surrounding the management and procedures of the Short Ballot Organization.[111] Aside from these rather perfunctory concerns of Wilson, Childs bore the primary responsibility for the success of the movement, and, along with his assistant, H. S. Gilbertson, he diligently carried on the campaign. After his involvement in presidential politics, Wilson was able to devote even less time to the short ballot movement, though Childs maintains that Wilson's interest remained as strong as ever.[112]

110. Richard S. Childs, "Woodrow Wilson Legacy," *National Municipal Review*, XXXXVI (January, 1957), 14-19.
111. Interview with the author, January, 1964.
112. Childs vehemently disagrees with Arthur S. Link's statement

In perusing Childs's papers on the short ballot movement and the short ballot *Bulletins* over that nine-year period, from 1911 to 1920, it is impressive to see the support obtained under Childs's direction. Backing was secured from groups across the political spectrum: labor unions, business organizations, farm organizations, mayors, governors, legislators, newspaper editors, and so forth. To list distinguished supporters is simply to repeat the names of the famous in the Progressive era. With Progressive contempt for "politicians," the renowned former President of Harvard, Charles Eliot, proclaimed, "It [the short ballot] is the gist of the whole matter—the only way to get rid of bosses and machines."[113] Among other illustrious figures of the day who gave their approval were Charles Evans Hughes; Governor Hiram Johnson, of California; Governor "Al" Smith, of New York; Louis Brandeis; Henry L. Stimson, cabinet officer; Elihu Root, also a cabinet officer; President Theodore Roosevelt; and President William Howard Taft, later Chief Justice of the Supreme Court.[114] With such dissimilar figures as Taft and

that "it [meaning the short ballot idea] was a short-lived craze with Wilson and he soon forgot the idea when he got into politics." Link, *op. cit.*, p. 126. Referring to a letter that he received from Wilson in 1919, Childs has written, "In that letter he wistfully lamented that his tasks elsewhere had denied him time for our crusade." Childs, "Woodrow Wilson Legacy," *National Municipal Review*, p. 14-19. Childs is confident that had Wilson survived his presidential years he could have secured his services as President of the National Municipal League, as he had with the National Short Ballot Organization. Interview with the author, January, 1964. Wilson had left to Childs's judgment the decision of merging the Short Ballot Organization with the National Municipal League in 1920. *Ibid.*

113. Richard S. Childs, "Peanut Politics and the Short Ballot," *Harper's Weekly*, LVIII (October 25, 1913), 23.

114. It is not to be inferred that Childs knew these particular persons intimately. Beyond the shared interest in the short ballot venture, the relationships were for the most part casual. Childs related that

Bryan rendering aid and comfort to the movement, it appears that Childs and his organization had truly achieved "nonpartisanship."

Has the short ballot movement been a "success?" From the outset, as noted previously, Childs had held, "Our national government has a Short Ballot—only three men to be selected by any one citizen."[115] Consequently, no "crusade" was needed at that level. As to the short ballot victories at the state and county levels, Childs himself admits that they have been modest.[116] However, at the municipal level the triumphs have been impressive because the principle of the short ballot was incorporated into the council-manager plan of local government, and this plan to date has spread to well over eighteen hundred American cities. As incorporated into the city-manager plan, the result has been a fairly resounding victory. Childs has explained: "The spread of the short ballot principle accompanies, of course, the city manager plan. *The two are inseparable.* In general the short ballot principle is now so well established that it is accepted as a matter of course as the foundation stone of centralized responsibility in government."[117]

The fusion of the National Short Ballot Organization with the National Municipal League in 1920 was

he met Theodore Roosevelt at the home of his father, who, as indicated, was a stanch Roosevelt supporter in the campaigns of 1912 and 1916. He observed at that meeting, because of the presence of "T. R.," there was "electricity in the air." Interview with the author, January, 1964.

115. Richard S. Childs, "What a Democracy Would Be Like," *Everybody's*, XXVI (March, 1912), 373. For a more recent statement, see Richard S. Childs, "Theories of Responsive Government Prove Practical," *Public Management*, XXIX (December, 1947), 356.

116. Childs, *Civic Victories*, pp. 88-89.

117. Richard S. Childs, "Along the Governmental Battle Front," *National Municipal Review*, XIX (January, 1930), 6. (Italics mine.)

not a symbol of failure—it simply represented the commencement of a new, and even more successful, phase in the short ballot struggle. From the vantage point of 1932, Childs could with accuracy write, "I was successful in making [the short ballot principle] the central feature of a new philosophy of political reform. . . . I was promptly off on a crusade that has kept me going ever since."[118]

This chapter has placed Childs within the intellectual ferment of the early decades of this century insofar as political movements are concerned. Admittedly, this sketch may appear superficial; nevertheless, the effort needs to be made because Childs reflects much of this period. In the subsequent chapters, as the specifics of his philosophy are brought into sharper focus and analyzed and evaluated, the spirit of pragmatism and Progressivism frequently appear, as do the doctrinal tenets of scientific management and its concomitant "principles" and "organizational-chart" approaches.

The short ballot movement has served as the capstone of this chapter for, in addition to being a highly significant facet in the unfolding of Childs's philosophy, it depicts him and his times in microcosm. The experimental and adventurous mood of pragmatism with its insatiable desire to "direct the struggle" (in this case against the bosses and their machines) is clearly present. Progressivism—with its yearning for a return to "democracy," with its scorn for "the politician," with its trust in the proper mechanical device to return government to "the people"—is also

118. Richard S. Childs, "What to Expect of Political Reform," *National Municipal Review*, XXI (June, 1932), 349.

manifested in the struggle for the short ballot principle. Above all, the zeal of Progressivism is found in
ample quantities in Childs's role in this crusade.[119]
Various facets of the scientific management school
are revealed in the short ballot venture, but most
significant is the acceptance of the belief that a "one-
best way" can be found. As evidence of the "principles approach," this one-best method turns out to be
the "Short Ballot Principle," which is immutable and
universal in its applicability. Finally, the "organizational-chart" (or mechanistic) approach, with its
emphasis upon problem-solving through a manipulation of the formal structure, is present in the short
ballot movement, for Childs and his ardent supporters
made it absolutely clear that a change in the form—
from the long to the short ballot—was *the* solution in
the road back to "democracy." All other aspects were
peripheral.

With this rudimentary foundation it is appropriate
to turn to a more detailed and comprehensive analysis
of Childs's ideal model of municipal government.

119. Plainly, considering the achievements of the short ballot movement, Childs's zeal was infectious. For evidence of this in book form,
see *The County: The Dark Continent of American Politics* (New York:
The National Short Ballot Organization, 1917) by H. S. Gilbertson,
who was Childs's assistant in the New York office of the National Short
Ballot Organization. In addition, see Albert M. Kales, *Unpopular
Government in the United States* (Chicago: University of Chicago
Press, 1914). Kales, a professor of law at Northwestern University,
probably had no peers in his fervor for the short ballot principle. He
wrote: "But as the fight for and against slavery was never settled till
slavery was abolished, so the war on politocracy will never cease till
some great national crisis has given birth to a new political philosophy
and a sound practice under it, which will sweep extra-legal government
from the field. That philosophy is summed up in three prosaic words:
The Short Ballot. They are the emancipation proclamation for our
government. The faithful and complete application of the principles
underlying the short ballot in our local and state governments will be
as important and perhaps as difficult a step for us to achieve as was
the emancipation of the slaves." *Ibid.*, pp. 262-63.

III

Childs and His Model
of
Municipal Government

> *"The difficulties of democracy ... are mechanistic, not moral, and respond to mechanistic corrections. ... It is the mechanism that makes the difference."* Richard S. Childs, 1955.[1]

With Progressive confidence in the individual and optimism in the democratic process, coupled with his long standing and unalterable belief that "human nature has not changed perceptibly since Adam,"[2] Childs sought to return to democracy through mechanistic manipulation, i.e., through the construction of a

1. Richard S. Childs, "Civic Victories in the United States," *National Municipal Review*, XXXXIV (September, 1955), 402.
2. Richard S. Childs, "Politics Without Politicians," *The Saturday Evening Post*, CLXXXII (January 22, 1910), 6. For a more recent statement reaffirming this attitude on 'human nature," see Childs "Civic Victories," *National Municipal Review*, p. 402.

machine model. In the first section of this chapter the analysis of the general nature of this model indicates that "the concept of democratics" and the inviolable "Three Rules" are the foundations upon which the model is erected. Childs's prescription of nonpartisan elections in municipal politics, dealt with in the second section, is indicative of his rejection of any political institution that is dysfunctional to the operation of a "smooth-running" machine. Specifically, he prescribes nonpartisan elections for local contests to eliminate the dysfunctional impact of national party participation in urban politics, and he assigns a limited role to "local parties" to promote an improved operation of the model. In the final section we come to the council-manager model that is the culmination of Childs's efforts. In addition to an analysis of the origins and development of this scheme, a detailed examination is undertaken of how this paradigm is to function according to the Childs design.

The "Machine Model"

In his construction of a machine model for local government, Childs assumes there are only two variables that affect the political process. One is "the people"; the other is the structure of government. On top of that assumption he places another, which embodies the belief that "the people" of New York, Chicago, Dayton, Cincinnati, and Kansas City have identical "characteristics," and that differences in political performances in these respective cities can be attributed to one factor—structure.[3] Characteristic

3. Richard S. Childs, *Civic Victories: The Story of an Unfinished Revolution* (New York: Harper and Brothers, 1952), pp. 3-5.

of the Progressive's use of the mechanical metaphor, Childs summed up the matter as follows: "Think of the people as you would of a brook when building a water mill! You would waste no time in deploring its lazy tendency to slip downward through every crevice in your dam; you would admit the fact and build a tight dam. . . . If your mill finally failed to work, you would still not blame the water but only the mill, and would strive to adapt its gearing to the force of the stream."[4]

Since the goal is democracy and the problem is mechanical, Childs seeks to construct a model governmental structure that will *perfectly* reflect the will of the electorate. In his words, "So the purpose of the modern technical attack has become that of making government more sensitive. . . . The object is democracy."[5] As would the engineer in the construction of a building, Childs has adhered to certain "fundamental principles" of design lest the edifice when completed have a faulty foundation. These basic tenets are contained in Childs's "concept of democratics."

The opening sentence of *Civic Victories* states, "There is no such word as 'democratics' but there ought to be, so we coin it now to describe phenomena produced when various mechanisms of government are provided for voters to operate."[6] In substance, the concept of "democratics" consists of "Three Rules," which are unassailable principles deserving universal application. These Three Rules provide the

4. *Ibid.*, p. 4.
5. Richard S. Childs, "Democracy That Might Work," *Century*, CXX (January, 1930), 13-14.
6. Childs, *Civic Victories*, p. xiii.

established norm, and any governmental form that deviates is to that extent structurally unsound.

"Rule One" is that *"elective offices must be visible."*[7] Underneath the new language is that familiar friend, the short ballot principle, "the foundation stone" of mechanically sound government. This rule commands that there be a limited number of candidates (preferably not more than five) appearing on the ballot and that the offices they seek be significant ones.

"Rule Two" requires that *"the constituency must be wieldy."*[8] This rule follows naturally from Rule One. The first rule, always the central point in Childs's thinking, stresses the importance of the *individual* candidate—the "one-best" man. The second rule becomes a necessary corollary to insure that the constituency does not become "so large in voting population that the task of canvassing it goes beyond the power of ordinary independent candidates and leaves a monopoly of hopeful nominations in the hands of permanent standing armies of organized political mercenaries."[9] Again, Progressive contempt for the "politicos" is manifested by such words as "mercenaries." To assure a wieldy constituency, the rule of thumb is, "Let the constituency be not so large but that an adequate impromptu organization can be put together at short notice!"[10]

In the large city (Childs sets 250,000 as the dividing point) the problem of the unwieldy constituency is most acute. To assure compliance with Rule Two in

7. *Ibid.,* p. 47.
8. *Ibid.,* p. 56.
9. *Ibid.*
10. *Ibid.,* p. 54.

metropolitan areas he urges proportional representation, for, as he reasoned as early as 1909, with "P. R.," "the candidate need only secure a quota instead of a plurality."[11] Throughout the years Childs has accepted the virtues of this device.[12] In 1952 he wrote, "P. R. provides the only dependable way of avoiding the sordid evils of ward systems without encountering the great partisan monopolies or binopolies characteristic of unwieldy constituencies (Rule Two)."[13]

"Rule Three" commands that *"governments must be well integrated."*[14] As the previous chapter has indicated, Childs and Progressivism in general sought democracy through simplified, unified, and integrated government. By 1955, Childs made this tenet of Progressivism one of his three inviolable rules. In that year he wrote that "superior democracy" will come only through "strengthened and simplified structures," and he continued: "Ramshackle mechanisms and needlessly numerous units are difficult for even the active participants to control. Still more difficult is it for the voters to control them. Intentionally or

11. Richard S. Childs, *Short Ballot Principles* (Boston: Houghton Mifflin Co., 1911), p. 58. For an explanation of how the required quota is computed, see Childs, *Civic Victories*, p. 248, or Ralph A. Straetz, *PR Politics in Cincinnati* (New York: New York University Press, 1958), p. 270.

12. John R. Commons and William Dudley Foulke in 1893 were among the first in America to expound the concept of proportional representation. C. G. Hoag became a fervent supporter in 1913, and more recently George H. Hallett has been the principal proponent. See Childs, *Civic Victories*, p. 242.

13. *Ibid.*, p. 248. Aside from the fact that it supplements Rule Two, Childs is impressed with the increased precision and symmetry that P. R. gives to his machine model. He "supports it as the ideal way to make policy-forming bodies truly representative," and he concludes, "Its virtues are mathematically provable." Childs, *Civic Victories*, pp. 246, 251.

14. Childs, *Civic Victories*, p. 70.

otherwise, they automatically frustrate the democratic process.''[15]

It is Childs's belief that from the properly constituted structural arrangements of government will flow the "public interest." This matter of the "public interest" is investigated more closely in the following chapter in the discussion of Childs and the Schubert schema; however, it is essential to indicate at this point that Childs conceives of his machine model as providing a canalization for the expression of the "will of the people," and *ipso facto,* he argues that the "public interest" is thereby served. If democratic procedures are followed, the "public interest" is to be defined, developed, and adopted automatically in a kind of input-output relationship. From the Childs viewpoint the larger purpose in building his model is to create an instrument that accurately and efficiently produces the "public interest."

In his pursuit of a mechanically perfect paradigm based upon these Three Rules, Childs found county government the epitome of "ramshackle government"; it was the antithesis of the standard prescribed by the rules. He explained, "Outside of New England with its township system there are 3049 counties which all violate Rule One and Rule Three and in some metropolitan and huge area counties . . . [Rule Two is violated also]."[16] By providing for numerous independently elected officials, who in turn are assigned responsibilities on the basis of an organization chart in complete disarray, Childs finds, "The County is thus an illustration of all the favorite American faults of government design, raised to the nth power.

15. *Ibid.,* pp. 69, 70.
16. *Ibid.,* p. 193.

It exhibits at its worst every one of the fallacies cherished by . . . the Jacksonian Democrats."[17]

In *Short Ballot Principles* in 1909, Childs had suggested that the solution to the "county problem" might lie in the abolition of county government.[18] As noted in the previous chapter, this radical idea caused some embarrassment to Woodrow Wilson. By 1913, Childs had developed a somewhat less drastic answer; he had produced a model for "a theoretically perfect county."[19] To begin with, this scheme would remove all sheriffs, judges, and district attorneys from county control and place them under state auspices. Also such matters as care of the insane and control of roads would be assigned to state jurisdiction. In sum, only "local affairs" (what these affairs are is not explicitly stated) would be left under county control, and the county-manager form of government, patterned after the city-manager form, would be instituted. Ultimately Childs proposed that the county Board of Supervisors should be removed from the ballot (in keeping with the short ballot principle), and instead of election, the Supervisors should be appointed by the respective cities of the county. Childs concluded, "we have left, so far as politics is concerned, no county at all! And that is your theoretically perfect county!"[20]

This chapter, as is Childs's career, is basically concerned with his erection of a model of municipal government; moreover, this emphasis upon his schema for county government is appropriate for considera-

17. *Ibid.*, p. 198.
18. Childs, *Short Ballot Principles*, pp. 98-99.
19. Richard S. Childs, "A Theoretically Perfect County," *The Annals of the American Academy of Political and Social Science*, XXXXVII (May, 1913), 274-78.
20. *Ibid.*, p. 278.

tion, for it brings into clear focus his preoccupation with a machine model, i.e., with the mechanics of politics. To him the county is the epitome of a "complex, rusty, instrument"[21] and is completely antithetical to the impeccable Three Rules and a "smooth-running" machine model.

In contrast to the "ramshackle" structure of the county, Childs offered the school board system as a mechanically correct design because it perfectly conforms to the Three Rules. He elucidated, "The elective school board with its professional appointive superintendent is ideal as to form—it has a short ballot of equally important board members, it is tightly and correctly integrated, and the district is usually wieldy."[22] This compliance with the Three Rules provides a "simple oneness" and a "unified organism."[23]

In between the two extremes of the county organization and that of the school board, Childs placed the systems of the national and state governments. In the case of the former he found it in general accord with the rules except on the matter of unwieldy constituency. This flaw Childs tended to dismiss as unavoidable, though the electoral college system, as designed, was a partial solution. As to the national government in general, he concluded, "Its structure should be left alone—the founders of the republic got

21. Richard S. Childs, "Ramshackle County Government," *Outlook*, CXIII (May 3, 1916), 44.
22. Childs, *Civic Victories*, p. 223. However, it is only with the form or internal organization of the school system that Childs is satisfied. He writes, "the facts remain that there are too many [school districts], that thousands of them should be consolidated . . . , that thousands more . . . can be acceptably and advantageously made appointive in municipal or county governments. . . ." *Ibid.*, p. 227.
23. Childs, *Civic Victories*, p. 66.

it pretty nearly right; the violation of [Rule Two] was not of their doing.''[24] Aside from increasing the appointive power of the Governor, and providing for an appointive state judiciary, the major structural change that Childs proposed at the state level was to provide for a unicameral legislature because "the dual structure violates Rule One and Rule Three.''[25]

The obvious omission from this discussion is Childs's appraisal of the compliance of council-manager government with the Rules. The city-manager plan is, of course, his major contribution, and, because of its overriding significance, is dealt with separately in a subsequent section of this chapter. It is sufficient to note at this point that about the city-manager plan Childs has written, "Here we come with our Three Rules to a scene of heartening victory. . . !''[26] As the manager plan is in complete harmony with the Rules, it represents the zenith of mechanical perfection.[27]

Banfield and Wilson have found that in Chicago the formal powers of the mayor, which are weak, have been greatly enhanced by the informal centralizing effect of the "boss' machine" (not to be confused with the "machine model").[28] As the authors have stated it, without "the organization" (meaning the

24. Richard S. Childs, ''Democracy That Might Work,'' *Century*, p. 16. Considering Childs's and Progressive opposition to the doctrine of separation of powers and the principle of checks and balances, it is of interest that Childs did not attack the federal structure as violative of Rule Three.

25. Childs, *Civic Victories*, p. 117. See also Childs, ''Democracy That Might Work,'' *Century*, p. 16.

26. Childs, *Civic Victories*, p. 141.

27. *Ibid.*, pp. 141-42.

28. Edward C. Banfield and James Q. Wilson, *City Politics* (Cambridge: Harvard and M. I. T. Presses, 1963), pp. 106-7. See also Edward C. Banfield, *Political Influence* (Glencoe, Illinois: Free Press, 1961), Chapter XI.

machine) the result can be "a weak and ineffective administration."[29] In brief, the authors are indicating the informal effect of the machine upon the formal political structure. This point is not original with Banfield and Wilson. In *Short Ballot Principles,* about one half-century earlier, Childs had revealed his awareness of this fact,[30] and in 1914 he wrote: "The government could not go on without [the political machines]. They have supplied a real deficiency in our governmental plan, *filling a gap.* . . . The politician has one of the hardest jobs in the world . . . in *applying the necessary cohesion to our ramshackle government* and keeping our impractical form of democracy, from collapsing altogether. . . ."[31] But it was Childs's contention that with the appropriate alteration in the formal structure and *mechanism* the need for the informal role of the boss and his "political machine" would end. He argued, "With the coming of the short ballot we shall see the end of [the boss'] work. He is an expert in citizenship, and on the short ballot basis there is nothing to be expert in. Good-by, old friend!"[32]

Nonpartisan Elections in Municipal Politics

The two major national political parties, as they have evolved in the American experience, Childs found dysfunctional to his design of municipal government. From his point of view, if the Three Rules are com-

29. Banfield and Wilson, *City Politics,* p. 107.
30. Childs, *Short Ballot Principles,* p. 130.
31. Richard S. Childs, *The Story of the Short Ballot Cities* (New York: The National Short Ballot Organization, 1914), p. 12. (Italics mine.) Woodrow Wilson made the same point in "Hide-and-Seek Politics," *North American Review,* CXCI (May, 1910), 588.
32. Childs, *The Story of the Short Ballot Cities,* p. 13.

plied with, there is no need for the intrusion of national parties (or organizations of their ilk) into local political affairs because the rules place the spotlight upon the individual candidate. Political organization obscures the individual candidate, impairs his freedom to adjudicate problems "on the merits," impairs the voter's freedom to choose among the various candidates, and results in a technically imperfect model.[33]

The role of the candidate in Childs's model of local government merits scrutiny because it accounts for his antipathy to extensive political organization in urban politics, and it explains the limited activity he assigns to "civic associations" in his model. He insulates his paradigm from extraneous and dysfunctional elements.

"Why" Childs has adhered to his uncompromising position that it is the individual candidate who counts, and designs his Three Rules accordingly, defies precise articulation. Partly his position stems from pragmatism's stress upon individualism and democracy, and, more particularly, it results from Progressive emphasis upon the individual's participation in the democratic process. Furthermore, and accentuated by Childs's lifetime confrontation with the Tammany machine, this position reflects the Progressive reformer's reaction to the "boss" and his

33. The primary concern in this analysis is with Childs's position on local political organization. Because of the inevitable problem of unwieldy constituency (Rule Two) in the gubernatorial and presidential races Childs has always conceded the need for parties at the state and national levels. At these levels Childs, in effect, accepts a doctrine of "responsible-party government." He is‑ impressed with the British party system, and urges the American political party to become "a great union of believers in certain principles." See Childs, *Short Ballot Principles*, Chapters IX, X; and Childs, *Civic Victories*, Chapter VIII.

"machine." To clear away the "clutter" of the "binopolistic" party structure in urban politics and to facilitate the "insurgency" of the municipal reformer, it became imperative and expedient to emphasize the role of the individual candidate.

In addition, scientific management would appear to have influenced Childs in this attitude. He modeled the manager plan in many respects on the pattern of the private business corporation, and, in further keeping with the spirit of Taylorism, he has great confidence in the role of the "expert" and the "efficiency" he can bring to municipal government. If urban government is primarily a matter of *expertise,* and is to considerable extent basically a business operation, which in the Childs schema it is,[34] then it follows, as Childs has consistently held throughout his career, that "obviously there could not, properly, be a Republican or a [Democratic] way of running"[35] local government. In sum, local government is not a proper concern of the great national parties, but is rather to be administered by the expert and overseen by the individual candidates. Finally, the mood of scientific management (plus perhaps a dash of Social Darwinism) is manifested in the selection of the respective candidates, since they are to compete on a man-to-man basis "on their simple merits,"[36] and the "one-best man" will triumph.

To insulate his model of urban government from the disruptive effects of the national party organiza-

34. In the strongest statement he has made on the matter, Childs wrote, "city government is nine-tenths business, with ordinance-making as a mere side-line." Richard S. Childs, "State Manager Plan," *National Municipal Review,* VI (November, 1917), 660.

35. Richard S. Childs, "Politics Without Politicians," *The Saturday Evening Post,* CLXXXII (January 22, 1910), 5.

36. Childs, *Civic Victories,* p. 180.

tions, Childs is a fervent expounder of the concept of nonpartisan elections. As a matter of simple legality, this device prohibits the appearance of party labels upon the ballot, and normally nomination for local office comes by *individual* petition. Within the non-partisan framework each candidate stands *alone* and exposed to "intensive public scrutiny." In addition, the national parties are rendered impotent, and the result is "politics without politicians."[37] There is, however, a restricted area within which Childs's design will tolerate local political organization.

It has often been difficult to ascertain with certainty whether the proponents of the nonpartisan election were objecting to partisanship per se at the local level or merely to national partisanship. In the case of Childs it is the latter proposition to which he objects.[38] In 1964 he has written, "The target of [the nonpartisan election] has been the local structures of the Republican and Democratic parties," and as to local parties he writes, "Non-partisan [*sic*] elections were never intended to forbid such organizations!"[39]

In general, however, Childs views local political organization with a suspicious eye, and he assigns it a minimal role within his over-all scheme. As the model stresses the individual candidate, the local political organizations ("civic associations," as he prefers to

37. Richard S. Childs, "500 'Non-Political' Elections," *National Municipal Review*, XXXVIII (June, 1949), 282.

38. In addition to believing that the national parties were impediments to the proper functioning of his model for local government, Childs accepts general reform doctrine that local politics has nothing in common with the state and national varieties and any union of the three is an unnatural one. For example, see Richard S. Childs, "Ballot Is Still Too Long!" *National Municipal Review*, XXXV (February, 1946), 70.

39. Richard S. Childs, "Non-partisan Elections in 14 Unwieldy Constituencies," 1964, p. 17 (mimeographed).

call them) are assigned the task of facilitating the participation of the single candidate in the electoral process. He concedes that this aid is necessary where there is a convergence of unwieldy districts (violation of Rule Two) and elections at large,[40] for in that eventuality the individual campaigner is denied full exposure to the electorate.[41]

Childs is not clear on "how" these "associations" are to promote man-to-man politics. In 1909 he implied that the local organization should not nominate candidates, but rather should focus as a "searchlight" on the various candidates that might arise.[42] Yet in 1964 he appears to be leaning toward acceptance of local "nominating organizations,"[43] and in the same manuscript he makes the strongest suggestion he has ever made for competitive party politics at the local level, with the comment, "And, in the big constituencies especially, [local parties] are needed to provide leadership, or competitive leaderships, in which could otherwise be chaotic scrambles and capricious outcomes."[44]

In any case, and this is the principal point, the Childs scheme makes the local party an adjunct of the individual's campaign. It is still "the man" that remains in the forefront of the electoral process. There is ample evidence in Childs's writings that he prescribes a local party which is a "de novo impromptu volunteer organization"[45] and which will be

40. The latter device Childs accepts as an essential ingredient in his schema to eliminate "the ancient evils" of the ward systems. Childs, *Civic Victories*, pp. 141-42.

41. Of course, the Childs model has provided for this contingency with proportional representation.

42. Childs, *Short Ballot Principles*, p. 87.

43. Childs, "Non-partisan Elections," p. 17 (mimeographed).

44. *Ibid.*

45. Childs, *Short Ballot Principles*, p. 79.

promptly "disbanded after the election."[46] The local party must be kept weak because the "impromptu insurgent"—the reformer—must always be free to rise, and, furthermore, once the candidate is elected to the council he must be a "free agent," a "free man," who is beholden to no "self-serving political go-betweens."

Perhaps the most positive contribution that the local party makes in Childs's model is to serve as an immunization for the local political community against "infection" from the national parties. In many cases, without the local associations, Childs warns, "the management of the local dominant national party may get tired of their hands-off position and realize that they can don a disguise and move back in."[47]

In the final analysis the Childs plan is constructed around individual candidacies, and since the participation of the national parties is dysfunctional of that end, the instruments of nonpartisan elections and local "associations" are incorporated into the machine model.[48]

46. Richard S. Childs, "Council-Manager Cities 1,000 Strong," *American City*, LXVI (January, 1951), 70. It is uncertain whether Childs would condescend to agree with Charles P. Taft that the local political organization ought to be maintained on a continuing and permanent basis. The article just cited, for example, would suggest not; however, there is recent evidence that he might. See Childs, "Nonpartisan Elections," (mimeographed). For Taft's position, see *City Management: The Cincinnati Experiment* (New York: Farrar and Rinehart, 1933), pp. 5, 235.

47. Childs, "Non-partisan Elections," p. 19 (mimeographed).

48. The dysfunctional concept, as an interpretive device in analyzing Childs's philosophy, is by no means applicable only in regard to his attitude on parties. Invariably when he rejects an element from his schema it is because in some way the element in question impedes the "smooth-running" of his machine. For example, in the ensuing section it will be seen that, in effect, this is his position on the doctrine of separation of powers. His attitude on parties was selected for discussion in this section not only to illustrate the notion of dysfunction but, in addition, because his views are of genuine significance in their own right.

The Council-Manager Model

Origins and Development

It is with the city-manager design that the culmination of Childs's contribution to the municipal reform movement is reached. "The new wonder," as Childs called it, was no dramatic departure from his earlier attitudes. Rather it represented the natural fruition of his philosophy.

The "Lockport Proposal," prepared by Childs with the assistance of Gilbertson, stated, "The Short Ballot—only five to elect, all of them important and conspicuous—is the gist of the plan."[49] As with the short ballot principle, the purpose of this new scheme, in keeping with Progressive antipathy for "the politician," was to foil the spoilsmen and their city machines. There are repeated examples in Childs's writings, similar to his comment to the *New York Times,* that *"the big accomplishment* of the council manager movement has been its success in demolishing local political machines in city after city."[50] As always, the ultimate goal is "politician-free democracy."

In the early years of the reform movement, Childs did accept the commission (or Galveston) plan, and, on occasion, in glowing terms.[51] In general, though, he

49. Richard S. Childs, *A Suggestion for an Optional Second Class Cities Law* (New York: n.p., n.d.), p. 3.

50. *New York Times,* January 31, 1932, p. 20 col. 1. (Italics mine.) Similarly, Childs has written, "My goal was the abolition of political bossism . . . ," and "It was to break up [the city machines] that the council manager plan was concocted and the diminished importance of political machines in cities where the plan is in effect is, to me, *the chief result of the movement."* Richard S. Childs, "City Manager Plan Will Endure," *American City,* LV (May, 1940), 36; Richard S. Childs, "What to Expect of Political Reform," *National Municipal Review,* XXI (June, 1932), 353. (Italics mine.)

51. For example, see Childs, *Short Ballot Principles,* pp. 66-67.

was always somewhat suspicious of the plan, and in 1912 he wrote, "Commission government is far from a perfect plan, and it only marks a transition toward better things, but it has the vital Short Ballot. . . ."[52] The latter point is revealing. Childs had accepted the commission plan because it served as an already existing vehicle for the transmission of his short ballot concept. Undoubtedly this was the principal factor in his initial endorsement of the plan. In addition to complying with Rule One (the short ballot principle), Childs observed, in harmony with Progressive thought, "The commission plan breaks with our old superstitions regarding the desirability of the separation of powers. . . ."[53] In brief, as Childs put it, the plan "like a new broom . . . sometimes swept dramatically clean. Unsound though it was, it cracked the assumption that the mayor and council plan was the only structure conceivable for the municipal government."[54] The stage was set for the "transition toward better things."

Childs's "transition" to the council-manager plan requires close examination. In 1913 he wrote an article entitled "The Theory of the New Controlled-Executive Plan," which laid the theoretical foundations for the shift from the mayor-council and commission forms.[55] To begin with, Childs found the fundamental "principles" upon which these two

52. Richard S. Childs, "What a Democracy Would Be Like," *Everybody's*, XXVI (March, 1912), 373.
53. Richard S. Childs, "Short Ballot and the Commission Plan," *The Annals of the American Academy of Political and Social Science*, XXXVIII (November, 1911), 151.
54. Richard S. Childs, "Half Century of Municipal Reform," *American Journal of Economics and Sociology*, XV (April, 1956), 323.
55. For Childs's earliest published reference to a city-manager plan see "What Ails Pittsburgh?" *American City*, III (July, 1910), 9-12.

forms were based structurally unsound. With regard to the mayoralty form he stated that it "overstrains our willingness to depend on the wisdom of one man."[56] He saw it as undemocratic because it confronted the electorate with the problem of "one-man power."[57] Furthermore, he declared that it "forks the line of responsibility."[58] Here, in consonance with Progressive sentiment, Childs rejected the separation of powers doctrine as applied to local government. In substance, his position was that this doctrine is dysfunctional to a "smooth-running mechanism"—it violates Rule Three; it produces "pulling and hauling, deadlocks, friction and delays, [and] trading of influence. . . ."[59]

In the case of commission government Childs found it defective because the "election of administrators is unsound in principle."[60] Subsequently, Childs implied that the commission form had an inherent dysfunctional element that causes the plan to violate Rule Three. That defect was the problem of "logrolling," for, as he reasoned, "when each commissioner had his pet department, logrolling for appropriations was a logical result . . . with nobody taking responsibility for the whole bill."[61]

In recent years Childs and the National Municipal League have reduced the whole case against the mayoralty and commission forms to one underlying cause. They have written: "Neither [form] has consistently provided good government. Both have

56. Richard S. Childs, "The Theory of the New Controlled-Executive Plan," *National Municipal Review*, II (January, 1913), 79.
57. *Ibid.*, p. 80.
58. *Ibid.*, p. 79.
59. *Ibid.*, p. 81.
60. *Ibid.*
61. Childs, *Civic Victories*, p. 137.

tended to produce poor executives and have furthered the spoils system. Why?

"Because both of these forms attempt to elect administrators to manage the city's business in denial of *the sound principle:* to choose qualified administrators, appoint; to find representative policy-makers, elect."[62] Most conspicuously Childs is reflecting the "principles approach."

In contrast, he expounded that the council-manager form conformed to "sound principles" of public administration. More specifically the new model was constructed upon the impregnable foundation of the Three Rules. Childs has explained: "[There is] compliance with Rule One—the short-ballot principle. Except in metropolitan cities, Rule Two re wieldy constituencies is not encountered. And Rule Three—integration—is completely respected since the single council holds in one place all the reins of power. ..."[63] In addition, the new scheme in the respective positions of the manager and council incorporated the "solid principle" of public administration, unanimously applauded during the Progressive years, that there could and should be a separation of politics and administration.

Finally, persistently throughout his career, Childs has stressed that the manager plan is consistent with the "principle of business organization."[64] Progressivism, scientific management, and public administration had accepted the model of the private business corporation as the form most likely to produce that

62. *The Story of the Council-Manager Plan* (New York: National Municipal League, 1962), p. 5. (Italics mine.)

63. Childs, *Civic Victories*, p. 142.

64. Richard S. Childs, "How the Commission-Manager Plan Is Getting Along," *National Municipal Review*, IV (July, 1915), 372.

prized commodity, "efficiency." Childs was no exception, and the Lockport Proposal stated, "The chief improvement in this [plan] over previous Commission Plans is the creation of this City Manager, thus completing the resemblance of the plan to the private business corporation with its well-demonstrated capacity for efficiency."[65]

Childs has never contended that the form per se of the manager plan was novel with him. In *Civic Victories* he has noted: "Although I am dubbed nowadays 'the father of the council-manager plan'...the principle is hardly novel enough to be patentable. Indeed, its structure is exactly that of over 80 per cent of our school boards, where the voters elect a small board which hires a professional superintendent who hires and directs the rest of the staff."[66] As the initial section of this chapter indicated, Childs considered the form of the school board the perfect example of a schema in conformity with the Three Rules—a faultless machine model.

With regard to the formulation of the plan, he prefers to explain his role as a ministerial rather than a paternal one. He has explained, "I was the minister who performed the marriage ceremony between the city-manager plan as first thought of in Staunton [Virginia], and the commission plan in Des Moines."[67]

65. Childs, *Optional Second Class Cities Law*, p. 2.
66. Childs, *Civic Victories*, p. 143. In 1911, Childs wrote, "The council-manager idea is of course not original with the Lockport people [meaning, in effect, himself] but is copied from the German system with its appointive mayor." See Richard S. Childs, "Lockport Proposal to Improve the Commission Plan," *American City*, IV (June, 1911), 286.
67. Richard S. Childs *et al.*, "Professional Standards and Professional Ethics in the New Profession of City Manager: A Discussion," *National Municipal Review*, V (April, 1916), 210. Childs and the National Municipal League have had over the years a running feud

In any event, the significant fact is that Childs pieced the council-manager plan together, gave it a rationale, and offered it as the major weapon in the "arsenal" of municipal reform. As Childs summed it up, "I am not saying that I did it all with my little hatchet, but neither will I deny the satisfaction that I get out of having seen my brain-child get up and walk away so promptly and vigorously!"[68]

To Childs with his considerable zeal and tenacity must certainly go the lion's share of the credit for getting the "brain-child" on its feet. In the summer of 1910 he instructed Gilbertson to draft the council-manager plan into statutory form whereupon it was presented to the New York State Short Ballot Organization for approval and sponsorship. Although in agreement with Childs's ideas, this organization declined sponsorship on the grounds that it could better devote its efforts to shortening the New York state ballot.

Undeterred, Childs took his scheme to the Board

---

with Staunton as to whether the council-manager plan commenced in Staunton or Sumter. In 1908 Staunton hired Charles E. Ashburner as a "general manager" to assist its mayor and the bicameral council. It was not until 1920 that Staunton adopted the orthodox council-manager design. For these reasons Childs and the League consider Sumter "the official birthplace" of the manager plan, and they consider Staunton only the "first city to have a city manager." This provoked the people of Staunton, and Childs reports, "The mayor of Staunton wrote bitterly year after year, to the National Municipal League Conventions, demanding recognition over Sumter as the pioneer. But in the careful silences, Staunton dropped out of sight and we went on talking about the Lockport plan, the Sumter plan, and later, the Dayton plan ... until the momentum of the movement was safely established and the correct charter form solidly crystallized." Richard S. Childs, "Theories of Responsive Government Prove Practical," *Public Management*, XXIX (December, 1947), 354.

68. Richard S. Childs, "Political Reform," *National Municipal Review*, p. 349.

of Trade of Lockport, New York, which was seeking to propose a new charter for that city. Convincing the Board of Trade of the soundness of his plan, Childs and Gilbertson, through their New York City offices, gave the measure extensive publicity. Ultimately, the New York state legislature ignored the proposal, but within another year came good news indicating that the well-executed advertising efforts were paying a rich dividend. Childs has related the story: "One glad day in 1912, when I came . . . to the . . . Short Ballot office, Gilbertson . . . had placed on the top of the incoming mail a telegram from the Chamber of Commerce of Sumter (pop. 8109) reporting that the South Carolina legislature had passed a bill submitting our plan to local referendum as an alternative to the regular commission plan. First Blood! Weeks later came news of its adoption, on June 12, three to one; the first commission was elected the same year and the plan took effect in January, 1913.''[69]

By the end of 1913 ten other cities had followed Sumter, and, as Childs states it, the plan was off "like a bunch of firecrackers!"[70] On January 1, 1914, Dayton, Ohio, then a city of slightly over 116,000, adopted the plan, and, Childs reminisces, "Politics went out the window when Dayton's first city man-

69. Childs, *Civic Victories*, pp. 145-46. Childs has stated that he played no specific role in the Sumter victory until after the South Carolina legislature had approved the plan and the people of Sumter had accepted it by referendum. In brief, his materials were used extensively in that crusade, but he was unaware that they were being used and he played no personal part. After acceptance of the plan, Childs did assist the new council in the preparation of an advertisement for a manager, and through his New York office he gave the ad nationwide distribution. These facts were confirmed in an interview with me, January, 1964. For a reproduction of the advertisement, see *ibid.,* p. 146.

70. Childs, *Civic Victories*, p. 147.

ager blew in. . . .'"[71] Throughout the years, Dayton has remained a showcase for the proponents of council-manager government. In 1915 the National Municipal League, which had accepted the strong mayoralty form but had never endorsed the commission plan, "came naturally to" the new scheme. With pride Childs has related that "[the] League rewrote its Model Charter to bring it into accord with the commission-manager plan and it became the orthodox ideal of the municipal reformers."[72] The ensuing spread of the plan over the past half century is history that need not be labored.

Before concluding this discussion on the origins, development, and spread of the council-manager form of government, it is essential to comment briefly on the political values to which it appealed. Don K. Price has oversimplified Progressivism, the municipal reform movement, and Childs in suggesting that the promotion of city-manager plan was primarily a "manipulation of symbols" by accomplished advertising men.[73] Progressive reformism, while revealing some of the advertiser's techniques, to be sure, was a broad and complex movement. Richard Childs was more than a "manipulator of symbols," though at times he was this,[74] and the establishment of manager government in Sumter and its subsequent spread were

71. *Ibid.*, p. 148.
72. *Ibid.*, p. 151.
73. Don K. Price, "The Promotion of the Council-Manager Plan," *Public Opinion Quarterly*, V (1941), 563-78.
74. An example of Childs as an advertising "manipulator" is seen in his observation, "We called [the scheme] the commission-manager plan at first to take advantage of the vogue for the commission plan and swerve the latter—a tactic which succeeded. The term 'council-manager plan' came in later years and is now the accepted name." Richard S. Childs, "The League's Second Stretch," *National Municipal Review*, XXXIII (November, 1944), 516.

more than Madison Avenue stunts. In its spread the manager plan appealed to an emerging set of values, in the opinion of this writer. This set of values is what Banfield and Wilson have called "the Anglo-Saxon Protestant middle-class political ethos."[75] Hofstadter has concisely described this ethos as follows: "[This system of values] founded upon the indigenous Yankee-Protestant political traditions, and upon middle-class life, assumed and demanded the constant, *disinterested* activity of the citizen in public affairs, argued that political life ought to be run, to a greater degree than it was, in accordance with *general principles* and *abstract laws* apart from . . . personal needs, and expressed a common feeling that government should be in good part an effort to *moralize* the lives of individuals. . . ."[76] In contrast to these values were those

75. Banfield and Wilson, *City Politics*, pp. 149-50.
76. Richard Hofstadter, *The Age of Reform: From Bryan to F. D. R.* (New York: Vintage Books, Inc., 1960), p. 9. (Italics mine.) Hofstadter's use of the adjective "disinterested" is apt because as Childs expounded the manager plan it was indeed to be impartial in application. The properly operating machine model in the Childs design would certainly allow no "political favoritism." In practice, even those who supported the adoption of the plan in their respective communities often violated this doctrinal tenet of impartiality. This occurred because some citizens "disliked in practice the impartial administration that they had admired in theory; there were many advocates of city manager government who wanted to cut out special privileges enjoyed by the politicians but looked on their own special privileges as inalienable rights." Harold A. Stone, Don K. Price, and Kathryn H. Stone, *City Manager Government in the United States: A Review after Twenty-Five Years* (Chicago: Public Administration Service, 1940), p. 109; also see generally Chapters 9 and 10 and p. 239. For further evidence that the doctrinal prescription of impartiality is violated by groups seeking access for their special interests, see Leonard D. White, *The City Manager* (Chicago: University of Chicago Press, 1927) p. 299, and Gladys M. Kammerer, Charles D. Farris, John M. Degrove, and Alfred B. Clubok, *The Urban Political Community* (Boston: Houghton Mifflin Co., 1963), particularly Chapters 2, 3, 4, 5, 8, and 9. In effect, these groups seek "personalized" government of

of the immigrant, the boss, and the machine, which have already been alluded to in the preceding chapter. Hofstadter has summed up this opposing value system: "[This] system, founded upon the European backgrounds of the immigrants, upon their unfamiliarity with independent political action, their familiarity with hierarchy and authority, and upon the urgent needs that so often grew out of their migration, took for granted that the political life of the individual would arise out of family needs, interpreted political and civic relations chiefly in terms of *personal* obligations, and placed strong *personal* loyalties above allegiance to abstract codes of law or morals."[77]

The manager plan, as promoted by Childs, was primarily attractive to "the Anglo-Saxon Protestant middle-class political ethos," and, concomitantly, as suggested in the previous chapter in the section dealing with scientific management, the plan had considerable appeal to the values of the business community. Because of the strength and opposing values of the city machines, Childs and those to whom his plan appealed had become, in the urban setting, "alienated voters."[78] This feeling of alienation resulted because these groups felt that they were "without influence" and "without power."[79] One can speculate that in the council-manager plan these groups possibly saw an institutional arrangement by

---

a kind suggestive of the urban immigrants' expectations of "personal services" from the boss' machine.

77. Hofstadter, *The Age of Reform*, p. 9. (Italics mine.)

78. On this general problem and the fact that there are several kinds or types of alienation, see Murray B. Levin, *The Alienated Voter* (New York: Holt, Rinehart and Winston, Inc., 1960). Chapter IV, "Political Alienation," is particularly relevant.

79. *Ibid.*, p. vii.

which they might offset the strength of the spoilsmen
and assert their own influence in municipal affairs.

The Functioning of the Model

Although Childs is usually tagged as the "father"
of the manager plan, Herbert Emmerich's choice of
the word "inventor" is perhaps more appropriate.[80]
At least metaphorically, it is more in keeping with the
use of the term, "the machine model." It has been
shown that upon a firm foundation of "proven principles" inventor Childs fashioned his paradigm of
municipal government. The nature of these incontrovertible laws has been reviewed. It is necessary to
analyze the machine itself and to examine its parts
and their respective functions.

Based upon the dichotomy of policy and administration, the two basic components of the manager
and the council are delegated specific functions.[81] The
mood of the "organizational-chart approach" hangs
heavy, and to promote the proper functioning of the
model Childs makes major role assignments. All
other roles in city governments are derivative from
these principal ones.

The striking element in the Childs conception of
the role of the council is the rationalistic symmetry,
the machine precision. As seen in the previous section, it was the individual candidate running in a nonpartisan election at large who was intensely scruti-
nized and chosen by "the people" as the "one-best
man." From this it follows in Childs's schema that
the commissioners "simply represent the people at

80. Letter to the author, January 13, 1964.
81. See Articles II and III of National Municipal League, *Model
City Charter* (New York: National Municipal League, 1941).

the City Hall.''[82] There is to be no "invisible government"—all government is to be carried on in "City Hall," and the rules and policies are to be made out in the open by the council only.

To insure minimum dysfunction, Childs is adamant that the council must function as a collective unit. To accomplish this end he insists that all members of the council be considered of equal stature—one spark plug can be of no more importance than another. Childs provides in his plan for a "mayor," which would seem to suggest a preferred status for that individual, but as Childs envisions the model, this is not so. In fact he has strongly dissented from the draft of the 1963-64 Model City Charter of the National Municipal League which provides for the "alternative" choice of a separately elected mayor.[83] In Childs's design the mayor, selected by the council, is no more than the "Chairman of the City Council" because "his powers [should be] merely those of chairman—no veto, no high salary, no separate appointive power over operating departmental employees," and for these reasons he should be called "Chairman" rather than "mayor."[84] Childs concludes, "Our use of the word 'Mayor' has been a mistake. . . . There is no mayor in the old sense in the manager plan. . . . The word 'Mayor' has become the seed of irrepressible deviations from the original intent of providing unification of powers in a *single*

82. Childs, *Optional Second Class Cities Law*, p. 2.

83. National Municipal League, *Model City Charter* (Tentative Draft) (New York: National Municipal League, 1963), Section 2.03.

84. Richard S. Childs, "Use of the Word 'Mayor' in the Model City Charter," 1963 (typed manuscript); and Richard S. Childs, "Separate Election of Mayors in the Council-Manager Plan," 1963 (mimeographed).

board."[85] Childs objects strenuously to the alternative proposal of the popularly elected mayor because the mayor "is actually, we hope, only a member of the council, [and] the moment anything sets him apart, you have a crack in the unity of the structure."[86] Childs still demands a council operating as an entity. If this unit is performing properly, the policy-making process of municipal government becomes remarkably simple and efficient according to Childs. He has reasoned: "The first job of reconstruction must be to integrate and unify the machinery of government. . . . Seek, therefore, unification . . . and allow all your elective officials to come together on an equal footing as a single body, thresh out their differences in [open, never closed] debate, and then end them all by the simple expedient of taking a vote, whereupon arguments cease and action begins."[87]

The first action of the new council when the plan is initially instituted is to select a city manager. As noted in Chapter II, the spirit of Taylorism surrounds this task, for a detailed procedure of selection is spelled out to guarantee recruitment of the "one-best man."[88] Among other things, those instructions warn

85. Childs, "Separate Election of Mayors," pp. 1-2 (mimeographed). (Italics mine.)

86. *Ibid.*, p. 3. Childs's visceral reaction to the "alternative" proposal on the ground that it causes a break "in the unity of the structure" may be well founded. For example, there is impressive empirical evidence that "separately elected mayors are a political hazard to managers," and that this procedure can "reduce [the] authority" of the manager or "at least . . . frustrate" him. See Kammerer *et. al.*, *The Urban Political Community*, p. 197, and Gladys M. Kammerer, "Role Diversity of City Managers," *Administrative Science Quarterly*, VIII (March, 1964), 442.

87. Richard S. Childs, "How to Work for Charter Reform," *American City*, VIII (February, 1913), 150.

88. Committee Report, "Suggested Procedure for Selecting a City Manager," *National Municipal Review* (Supplement), XXII (December, 1933).

that the council should let prospective candidates know that it "will observe scrupulously the principles of council-manager government."[89] In brief, the manager and the council must agree to accept their respective role assignments in order to insure that the mechanism will operate at maximum efficiency.

Childs has written extensively on the role of the manager in his schema, and no facet has caused him greater difficulty or eluded him more than this one. The problem will be dealt with in considerable detail in the ensuing chapters, and at this juncture it will suffice to state the model role of the manager. Basic to the Childs paradigm is a vision of the manager as an "administrator." This idea, of course, stems from the policy-administration dichotomy with the council performing the former function and the manager the latter. Because of his administrative status the manager is an "expert" and "professional." He is to conduct himself (and to be treated) accordingly. He is the conduit through which council policy passes and is executed. As Childs states it, "He has no authority to seek or interpret orders from the people direct—*only* through the commission."[90] Furthermore, in this process the council acts "as a body. Individual members should never give orders to the manager or to his subordinates."[91] In sum, "the idea is that the council is to act always as a whole and stick to policy and the manager is not to govern but to administer."[92] This

89. *Ibid.*, p. 5.
90. Richard S. Childs *et al.*, "Professional Standards and Professional Ethics in the New Profession of City Manager: A Discussion," *National Municipal Review*, V (April, 1916), 198. (Italics mine.)
91. Richard S. Childs *et al.*, *Best Practice with the Manager Plan* (New York: National Municipal League, 1963), p. 4.
92. Childs, *Civic Victories*, p. 171.

procedure will assure that the machine model will run with minimum friction.

Childs has not deviated from the conclusion he made in 1915 that: "The position of city manager, of course, is the central feature of the plan and the ultimate theory of the scheme contemplates that he should be an expert in municipal administration, selected without reference to local politics, and even imported from out of town. . . . The transferability of managers from city to city also is an established fact."[93] Because of his *expertise* and his status as an "outsider," the manager within Childs's scheme acquires that characteristic of "transferability." In a sense he becomes an interchangeable cog fitting many municipal machine models.

To maintain this desired element of transferability the manager "must at all cost keep out of politics."[94] Childs has contended that this is "a most important thing to the development of a smoothly running mechanism."[95] To Childs in 1915 "keeping out of politics" depicted the manager "crawling into a hole out of the limelight and resolutely staying there, and thus unobtrusively continuing as manager through successive administrations no matter how various may be the commissions that come and go over his silent head."[96] As of 1963 Childs has not substantially

93. Childs, "How the Commission-Manager Plan Is Getting Along," pp. 373-74.

94. *Ibid.*, p. 380. The Sumter ad for a manager, which Childs assisted in preparing, stated, "There will be no politics in the job; the work will be purely that of an expert." Quoted in Childs, *Civic Victories*, p. 146.

95. Richard S. Childs, "The Principles Underlying the Plan," in *Commission Government with a City Manager* (New York: The National Short Ballot Organization, 1914), p. 15.

96. Childs, "How the Commission-Manager Plan Is Getting Along," *National Municipal Review*, p. 380.

changed this view: "[The manager] should always keep in mind his subordination to a council's decision. He should never promote or defend policy publicly until it has been adopted by council. . . . He should not thrust himself or let himself be thrust by the council into the limelight. . . . [He] should play no part in election campaigns, supporting candidates or identifying himself with any of the community's parties or factions."[97]

It is at this juncture that Childs's paradigm seems to manifest ambivalence at best, and inconsistency at worst. For though the manager, as "administrator," is to eschew "politics" scrupulously, at the same time he is to provide "policy initiation" or "community leadership." These latter elements are described as follows:

[The manager] has the responsibility to assess the impact of [new] broad trends on local government and to invent solutions and adaptations for consideration by the council. He should encourage it to decide positively instead of passively accepting his recommendations. . . .

The manager's portion of community leadership consists mainly of bringing to council members and the community an awareness of present and future problems and alternative solutions.

By increasing his skill in dealing with people—his council, municipal employees, the press and the public—he continues the official's traditional role of guiding and directing public affairs.[98]

97. Childs *et al.*, *Best Practice*, p. 6.
98. *Ibid.*, pp. 6-7. For earlier evidence that Childs viewed the manager as vastly more than a mere policy-executing eunuch, see Richard S. Childs, "What the City Manager of Klebubudaydoc Did," in the *City Manager Association Yearbook* (Clarksburg, West Virginia: City Manager Association, 1921), pp. 196-97; White, *The City Manager*, p. 149; Richard S. Childs, "Rise and Spread of the City Manager Plan of Local Government," *American City*, XXXXIII

Patently the role of the manager in the Childs design is elusive, though, as with the council, it is elaborately spelled out. It is a troublesome issue and will be explored in depth in the following chapters; however, the manager's role with all of its apparent ambivalence or inconsistency is part of the formal model.

The final feature in the model role of the manager relates to his tenure. This facet is also best understood as an adjunct to a machine design. In denying the manager protected tenure Childs reasons, "But any device which so protects the tenure of the city manager as to enable him conceivably to defy or flout a majority of the representative council impairs the unity and discipline of the governmental mechanism and is utterly unsound in principle.'"[99] In short, protected tenure, because of "impairing" the "mechanism," would be a dysfunctional element.[100]

Aside from role assignments to the council and the manager to insure an efficient and quiet-running machine, Childs also apprises the voters and the press on their conduct in order to guarantee maximum proficiency for all elements in the community. Childs has

---

(September, 1930), 132. For additional recent evidence, see Richard S. Childs, "The Enduring Qualities of a Successful Manager," *Public Management*, XXXXV (January, 1963), 2-4.

99. Childs, *Civic Victories*, pp. 184-85. See also Richard S. Childs, "No Tenure for City Managers," *National Municipal Review*, XXXVIII (April, 1949), 167-70. For early evidence of Childs's rejection of protected tenure for the manager, see Childs, "How the Commission-Manager Plan Is Getting Along," *National Municipal Review*, p. 377.

100. Childs approves of the procedural safeguards set forth in Article III of the *Model City Charter* concerning removal of the manager. These provisions are not extensive and, in substance, the manager serves at the pleasure of the council. He approves of these minimum safeguards to allow the public time to mobilize "when the contemplated removal has been believed to be based on political motives." Childs, "No Tenure for City Managers," *National Municipal Review*, p. 170.

not deviated substantially from his 1933 instruction that "the voters should not adopt the council manager plan if they want political or party government. Politics and this plan will not mix."[101] More recently he has advised, "This is the voters' responsibility: to elect people who best understand and represent a city and *who understand and support the plan.*"[102] In essence, the voters should support those candidates who best understand how the mechanism functions and their role in its operation.

As to the role of the press, Childs has been very explicit: "The press should encourage the mayor and council [rather than the manager] to do the talking since the mayor and council determine all policies.

"The press should refrain from overdramatizing the city manager. . . . Let the manager keep out of the limelight. . . .

"The reckless, sneering press [must avoid] driving out citizens of the superior type [who run for the council]."[103] Thus a properly "disciplined" press can also assist greatly in making the model work.

If the paradigm fails to work as described, Childs offers a list of possible explanations. It is noteworthy that these items are extraneous to the structure of the ideal type. For example, he has observed, "Sometimes defects in charters—variations from the Model Charter—[lead] to disorder in administration."[104] If the structure in a given community is "orthodox" and

101. Richard S. Childs, "The Best Practice Under the City-Manager Plan," *National Municipal Review*, XXII (January, 1933), 41.

102. Childs *et al.*, *Best Practice*, p. 1. (Italics mine.)

103. Childs, "The Best Practice Under the City-Manager Plan," *National Municipal Review*, pp. 41-42. For recent evidence that Childs may have assigned a more flexible role to the press, see Childs *et. al.*, *Best Practice* p. 3.

104. Childs, *Civic Victories*, p. 176.

still a "smooth-running mechanism" fails to result, then the trouble might be found in "the courthouse crowd [which provides] the base ... for every sneering attack upon the city manager and his nonpolitical administration."[105] Thus culpability may lie with the ousted "politicians." On the other hand, according to Childs, the difficulty may stem from the failure of the manager or the council (or perhaps the voters or the press) to have played their assigned roles faithfully. The manager, having inherited a "mediocre council," may have "[fallen] into the way of making policy"[106] because of the failure of his council to do so, i.e., to play its role, or the problem may be simply that the manager has "a lively sense of headlines" and, therefore, is not playing his prescribed role.[107] In any case it is not the ideal model that is defective, but rather outside variables are causing the mechanism to function improperly, and it is to those factors that the trouble shooter should direct his efforts.

In his preoccupation with the mechanistic model, Childs reflects many aspects of the intellectual movements analyzed in the preceding chapter. He reveals the pragmatist's faith that man can manipulate the events; there is no pessimistic determinism. In addition, Childs shares the Progressive's considerable zeal, and he is a participant in the Progressive pursuit of the correct mechanical device to restore "true democracy" and to thwart the "boss." Also Childs manifests the Progressive preferences for strongly integrated government and the separation of policy and administration, and he reflects Progressivism's

105. *Ibid.*, pp. 195-96.
106. *Ibid.*, p. 158.
107. *Ibid.*, p. 159.

distrust of the doctrine of separation of powers.
Finally, in the development and promotion of his
council-manager model, it was noted that Childs's
scheme appealed to the emerging values of "the
Anglo-Saxon Protestant middle-class political ethos."

The Three Rules are clear evidence of a "principles approach," while the "theoretically perfect
county," along with the whole concept of council-manager government, are solid examples of the "organizational-chart approach," wherein the achievement of
reform is to be found in the formal organization.

The scientific management school is prominent in
the Childs model. The idea of a machine model,
coupled with the problem of the dysfunctional, is a
chapter out of Taylorism, as is the persistent concern
with the "expert," the "technical," and the "structural." Regarding Progressivism's and Taylorism's
penchant for "efficiency," Childs looked for a governmental design that would give "harmony" and "efficient low-frictional action."[108] In short, he searched
for the "one-best way." To assist in achieving this
end he employed the "one-best-man" approach in the
selection of the council and the manager.

Based upon his "concept of democratics," Childs
has had unshakable faith in his erection of a machine
model, for he is convinced, "It is the machine that
makes the difference."[109]

108. Childs, *Short Ballot Principles*, p. 122.
109. Richard S. Childs, "Civic Victories in the United States," *National Municipal Review*, XXXXIV (September, 1955), 402.

IV

Critique of the Model: The Essence of the Closed System

"We need [not] revise our fond a priori theories of yesteryear!" Richard S. Childs, 1940.[1]

The previous chapter revealed that Childs has built a rationalistic machine model, which is "ideal" in the Platonic sense and not in the sense used by modern empiricists for purposes of conceptualization. Essential to an understanding of Childs's philosophy is a realization that his utopian model represents a closed system, and it is with the origins of this fact that this chapter is occupied. In the succeeding chapter the implications of this fact are explored. Moreover, because the present chapter is concerned with matters of critique of the essence of the closed system, the

1. Richard S. Childs, ''The City Manager Plan Passes Its 'Exams,' '' *National Municipal Review*, XXIX (July, 1940), 444.

schema of Glendon Schubert has been utilized as an additional tool in analyzing and understanding Childs's paradigm.[2]

The Closed System

The Childs system is a closed one because in its initial construction all factors are accounted for and no others are allowed subsequently to intervene. The result is a schema that is impervious to change or alteration. In Childs's thinking his system represents the culmination of the municipal reform movement. With his customary zest Childs concludes *Civic Victories* with this pronouncement:

There stands the panorama of the program of the modern political reformer! There is no competing school of thought, no contrary program. You will find it scattered through every university textbook on government and even in high-school texts, stated with approval but with less completeness and urgency. Opposition appears only when the program encounters in specific battles the self-serving sputter of local beneficiaries of needless complex "democratics." But this book is the first documented statement of *the whole uncontested creed.*[3]

This aura of finality, also characteristic of the scientific management movement and the "principles approach" generally, has been a persistent theme throughout Childs's thinking. For some time he has believed that the council-manager plan is "now long

2. Glendon Schubert, *The Public Interest: A Critique of the Theory of a Political Concept* (Glencoe, Illinois: Free Press, 1960).
3. Richard S. Childs, *Civic Victories: The Story of an Unfinished Revolution* (New York: Harper and Brothers, 1952), p. 278. (Italics mine.)

past the testing period,"[4] and he has happily concluded, "It is nice to think that reformers can call something finished and leave it alone thereafter!"[5]

To Childs the task that remains is twofold. On the one hand remains the unfinished job of spreading the council-manager plan to all cities in the nation,[6] while, on the other, is the need to preserve the "orthodoxy" of the plan. On this latter point Childs approvingly notes, "For a third of a century now the council-manager movement has been kept true to the original concept and few of the hundreds of local charter commissions have diverged into serious errors of principle."[7]

Childs is confident that the opponents of the manager plan cannot withstand the force of the movement. He reasons, "[The] program [is] unchallenged nowadays by any but the characters who comprise its

4. *Ibid.*, p. 156. For examples of earlier evidence that the system had closed, see Richard S. Childs, "A New Civic Army," *National Municipal Review*, X (June, 1921), 327; and, Richard S. Childs, "The Rise and Spread of the City Manager Plan of Local Government," *American City*, XXXXIII (September, 1930), 131.

5. Richard S. Childs, "City Manager Government," *National Municipal Review*, XXV (February, 1936), 50. In 1963, Alfred Willoughby, executive director of the National Municipal League, wrote, "Alone among the forms of government . . . , the council-manager plan has won the virtually unanimous approval of political scientists . . . as the most workable in United States communities." Richard S. Childs *et al.*, *Best Practice with the Manager Plan* (New York: National Municipal League, 1963), Foreword.

6. Richard S. Childs, "The Rise and Spread of the City Manager Plan of Local Government," *American City*, XXXXIII (September, 1930), 131. Perhaps with more seriousness than humor Childs wrote in 1962, "Extrapolating the current rate of growth of the council-manager plan, it appears that in another twenty years the plan will be universal in the United States. I have planned accordingly to take my pills and last that long. . . ." Richard S. Childs, "Fifteenth Annual Report of the Guest Artist," November, 1962, p. 3 (typed manuscript).

7. Childs, *Civic Victories*, p. 178. A notable exception is the fact that about one-half of all council-manager cities provide for a mayor selected by the electorate rather than the council, and, as noted in the previous chapter, Childs greatly regrets this deviation.

targets."⁸ These "characters" are, of course, "the politicians." As to any academicians who may attempt to undermine the "uncontested creed" he is equally as certain that the momentum of the plan will sweep them aside.⁹

It is significant that with his closed system Childs has diverged from the spirit of pragmatism. At the outset he shared its mood of experimentation, and this, of course, contributed to the spirit of reform of the Progressive era. However, once his manager plan had been conceived, adopted in Sumter as he designed it, and begun its spread across the continent Childs lost his experimental temperament. He believed that the "principles" had been firmly established. Contrary to all that Jamesian pragmatism stood for, he had found "truth" with a capital *T*.

Why has the Childs system been a closed one? Such closure is not inconsistent with the scientific management school in its search for immutable and universal "principles" that would afford the "one-best way," which, in itself, had an air of conclusiveness surrounding it. Since Childs shared much of the spirit of this approach, not surprisingly, he reflected this mood. Yet with Childs this response is too facile. The answer lies deeper.

Childs's model is built on utopian theory. Like Plato's system, his model is an "ideal" in the normative sense. It represents a perfected goal, and all political efforts should be directed to its acceptance and installation. This conception of a model stands in marked contrast with that used by the causal theo-

8. Richard S. Childs, "Citizen Organization for Control of Government," *The Annals of the American Academy of Political and Social Science*, CCLXXXXII (March, 1954), 133.

9. Interview with the author, January, 1964.

rists who employ models to describe a generally prevailing average set of relationships of a number of phenomena. The model of the causal theorists is not, of course, a normative one for which one "ought to" strive. Rather, it serves as an analytic tool, as a point of departure, in describing and understanding the "real" world of human behavior.

Alteration or change of any model requires a strong empirical or causal theory as a supplement, which will reveal inadequacies of the ideal paradigm.[10] Childs's system remains sealed because he does not possess a vigorous empirical theory and training in modern empirical method. This void is attributable to his view of the world of politics and administration. It is with this conception that the following three subsections are concerned.

Childs and the Group Theory of Politics

It is of interest that *Short Ballot Principles* was written in 1911, three years after Arthur Bentley wrote his classic, *The Process of Government*. Although Childs and Bentley were both products of the Progressive revolt, their respective views of the world of politics were quite dissimilar. Bentley was virtually ignored by the political scientists and political commentators of that day. He was ahead of his time. In contrast, Childs, very much in keeping with the thought forms of the era, found a more receptive audience.

Childs could not agree with Bentley that "the society itself is nothing other than the complex of the

10. I have used the terms "empirical" and "causal" interchangeably.

groups that compose it.''[11] At least he could never accept the premise that it is out of the group struggle that the ''public interest'' will arise. In Childs's schema the interest group is anathema to the ''public interest,'' and because of this must be expunged from the body politic. In essence Childs pictures, as did many Progressives, two competing groups in the political realm: ''the people'' and ''the politicians.'' To a large extent his model is constructed upon this premise; it is designed to defeat the politician and to manifest ''the will of the people.'' The latter concept Childs envisions as more monolithic than variegated.[12]

It is true that proportional representation manifests to some extent an awareness of, and a concession to, the group theory of politics; however, there would be danger in pressing this point too far. In the first place this is the only major evidence of Childs's cognizance of the group struggle.[13] In the broad

11. Arthur F. Bentley, *The Process of Government* (Bloomington, Indiana: Principia Press, 1949), p. 222.

12. The Childs version of the ''will of the people'' is suggestive of Rousseau's ''General Will.'' In Childs's philosophy the appropriate governmental machinery will spring this sentiment loose. Childs manifested this attitude in his first published article (see ''The Short Ballot,'' *Outlook*, LXXXXII [July, 1909], 635-39), and he has adhered faithfully to it throughout his career.

13. Don K. Price has reported that the American Proportional Representation League, which was founded in 1893, ''worked for twenty-two years without effect, until it began to concentrate its efforts on cities considering the manager plan.'' Don K. Price, ''The promotion of the Council-Manager Plan,'' *Public Opinion Quarterly*, V (1941), 576. In 1915 the Proportional Representation League, though not formally merging with the National Municipal League, scored a big victory by securing the incorporation of ''P. R.'' into the *Model City Charter*. As Childs related, ''. . . P. R. had to wait until the little council-manager movement had become strong enough not to be sunk by so novel and unfamiliar a supplement.'' Childs, *Civic Victories*, p. 242.

Although Childs has been a consistent supporter of proportional representation, he has not promoted it with the relish that he has pro-

sweep, his writings are not preoccupied with a group theory—P. R. must stand alone. Secondly, in Childs's thought the group conflict which is acknowledged is subsidiary to the main struggle between "the self-servers and the good-government forces." Group conflict is not conceived as taking place among the "good government forces" themselves. In Childs's system there is the underlying belief that if the proper design is followed, the group conflict within the "good-government forces" will cease. That is, "the people" with the proper machinery will and can act *in unison* because the ideal model will produce results over which rational and reasonable men can not differ. In short, the perfect state of equilibrium is possible of attainment.

During the heyday of Progressivism, Childs had maintained that with the appropriate scheme or structure "pulling and hauling, deadlocks, friction and delays, [and] the trading of influence" would cease.[14] In more recent years he has offered Dayton, Ohio, as the classic case of a community coming into practically a perfect state of equilibrium because of many years of faithful following of the manager plan. He notes that in that city the municipal elections have become "tame, even perfunctory" because "there are commonly no issues, no outs disparaging the ins, making charges and countercharges. . . ."[15] In brief, "There's nothing in sight to stir anybody's emotions."[16] Childs points out that the Citizen's Com-

moted his council-manager plan and its supporting devices, such as nonpartisan elections.

14. Richard S. Childs, "The Theory of the New Controlled-Executive Plan," *National Municipal Review*, II (January, 1913), 81.

15. Richard S. Childs, "It's a Habit Now in Dayton," *National Municipal Review*, XXXVIII (September, 1948), 421.

16. *Ibid.*

mittee, the organization of the "good-government forces," has atrophied over the years, but he is quick to add, "It was not waning vigor or alertness—there was no need to do more."[17] Childs is pleased to find that in Dayton there is "no trading or stipulations with party leaders," and, he happily writes, "Political strife becomes virtually extinct as voters continue to elect 'citizen' candidates to city council."[18] In this city he finds that "decency and serenity" prevail, and he concludes, "Happy is the land that has no history."[19] In Childs's analysis Dayton, because it has adhered to the manager model, is like a gyroscope in a state of suspension; the group struggle is conspicuous for its absence.

Childs's perception of the politics of Dayton is an excellent illustration of his conception that group conflict is not a central feature of the political process. Moreover, his conception of Dayton suggests he may be ignoring what Schattschneider has called "the mobilization of bias."[20] It is Schattschneider's thesis that within the American political context "organized, special-interest groups" constitute a "pressure system."[21] He postulates that these groups represent "a mobilization of bias in preparation for action."[22] Finally, Schattschneider concludes, "The business or upper-class bias of the pressure system shows up everywhere."[23] Schattschneider's hypotheses suggest

17. *Ibid.*, p. 424.
18. *Ibid.*, p. 421.
19. *Ibid.*, pp. 426, 427.
20. E. E. Schattschneider, *The Semi-Sovereign People* (New York: Holt, Rinehart and Winston, 1960), p. 30. See particularly Chapter II, "The Scope and Bias of the Pressure System."
21. *Ibid.*, p. 29.
22. *Ibid.*, p. 30.
23. *Ibid.*, p. 31.

that in reality what may have happened in Dayton is that because of the structure afforded by the Childs model the business community may have gained access to and domination of Dayton politics to the exclusion of other groups and interests. Childs himself concedes "the prolonged domination of Dayton by its businessmen," but, in effect, he defends this consequence as merely a manifestation of voter preference (i.e., "the public will").[24] When one group dominates political decisions the superficial appearance can be that of a bland, issueless politics of the type Childs found in Dayton, but beneath the surface the reality may not accord with the appearance. If there is an incongruity between the appearance and the reality, Childs would be unlikely to detect it because of his conception of group conflict.

Allied to Childs's conception of the group struggle is his perception of that phenomenon often called "politics." As was characteristic of many of his Progressive cohorts, Childs considered the word "politics" an epithet connoting the unsavory machinations of the "boss."[25] Not surprisingly, as a corollary, the "good-government forces" were violently opposed to "politics." It might be argued that this is an unduly restrictive use of the word. Nevertheless, if the narrow definition employed is made clear, there can be no quarrel. The problem is, however, more serious than this.

Beyond the initial struggle with the politicos, Childs and others of the Progressive vintage in their

24. Childs, "It's a Habit Now in Dayton," *National Municipal Review*, p. 427.

25. In his first article, Childs wrote, "The very word 'politician' has a special meaning of reproach in this country which foreigners do not attach to it." Childs, "The Short Ballot," *Outlook*, p. 637.

view of the political world do not conceive of politics as a processual phenomenon.[26] This phenomenon may be described, among other ways, as "who gets what, when and how" or as "the authoritative allocation of values for a society."[27] But the matter of precise definition is not important. Rather it is the concept that counts.[28]

Because he does not see group conflict over the "authoritative allocation of values," Childs does not view politics as a continuing process. Where Bentley and his intellectual heirs, such as the behavioralists, depict politics as a matter of process, dynamics, flux, and continuing change,[29] Childs, and kindred theorists, view it as a static, structured, and formalistic matter. The former visualize politics as a state of developing, the latter, as a state of being. Childs in his analysis of Dayton presents a classic example of the traditionalist description of politics in a static state of being. It is symbolic of the conflict between the "new" and the "old" political science that in 1908 Bentley should be writing of "process" and in 1911 Childs should be expounding on "principles."

For his utopian system to remain open and viable, it was essential that it be accompanied by empirical theory. Yet, because Childs has not accepted the group concept and its emphasis upon politics as a matter of continuous change, and instead looks to the

26. Childs first reveals this position in *ibid.*

27. See Harold D. Lasswell, *Politics, Who Gets What, When, How* (New York: McGraw-Hill, 1936), and David Easton, *The Political System* (New York: Alfred A. Knopf, 1960), 129.

28. When Childs does appear to approach the political realm of process, he will speak of "community leadership," of "guiding and directing public affairs," or of "civics" rather than of "politics."

29. In urban politics this would be reflected in policy conflict over such matters as land use, zoning, tax rates, urban renewal, and racial policy.

world of static politics he found in Dayton, he has no necessity for such theory. For if the properly installed ideal model abates the group conflict and the continuing process it connotes, and if there is no substantial change (or conflict) through time, there is no need for causal theory. Childs does not go back of the equilibrium he describes to find out what groups or factions rule Dayton in the fashion he describes, why they so rule, and to what extent "issues" are not allowed to emerge to cause conflict that would disrupt the statics. The "mobilization of bias" or the "power structure" of a council-manager city are alien to his concepts. There is no requirement to test empirically the model's adaptation to change because there has been no change and no departure from specifications.

Childs and Organizational Theory

Another reason for the absence of causal theory in Childs's system is his acceptance of traditional organizational theory. This attitude was discussed in Chapter II as one of the foundations of Childs's philosophy. As seen, his construction of a machine model owes much to the traditional theories of organization and their stress of the formal structure. There is no intent to belabor that point further in this section. The factor to be emphasized here is that because of Childs's organizational theories, his system makes no demand for empirical theory, and, as a consequence, is closed.

Traditional or classic American organization theory,[30] of which Childs is an unquestionable mani-

30. See, for example, Luther Gulick and Lyndall Urwick (eds.), *Papers on the Science of Administration* (New York: Institute of Public Administration, 1937).

festation, developed independently of the theories of Max Weber, yet there are remarkable similarities between the Weberian and traditional American approaches, and for this reason the Weberian model is useful as a tool of analysis. In the case of Childs the similarity between his model of municipal government and the Weberian bureaucratic "ideal type" is striking.

Both men conceive of the administrative process as principally a matter of the formal organization.[31] There are neat lines of hierarchy and fixed and official jurisdictional areas regulated by clearly established and rationalized rules and regulations. To illustrate, consider Childs's role assignments to the manager and the council. Furthermore, both men place the full-time appointive career expert in a central role in their respective systems. This emphasis is reflected in Weber's employment of the civil servant of the European system and in the role Childs assigns to the manager. No attempt will be made to exhaust the comparison as to specifics. Suffice it to say that both men offer formal rationalistic bureaucratic models, which, and this is the important point for present purposes, make causal theory unnecessary and irrelevant.

There is no need for such theory because all of the focus is upon the formal apparatus. The matter of the informal organization and its impact upon the formal structure is virtually ignored.[32] For example, in the

31. For Weber's position, see Max Weber, *Theory of Social and Economic Organization*, trans. A. M. Henderson and T. Parsons (New York: Oxford University Press, 1947), particularly pp. 333-36.

32. For classic studies indicating the importance of the informal organization, see F. J. Roethlisberger and W. J. Dickson, *Management and the Worker* (Cambridge: Harvard University Press, 1939), and Chester I. Barnard, *The Functions of the Executive* (Cambridge: Harvard University Press, 1938).

Childs schema no attention is paid to the problem of tensions between the manager as a general administrator and the professional specialists working under him. This problem of conflict between the "generalist" and the "specialist" is a real one to those cognizant of the importance of the informal organization.[33] To study that elusive "thing" called informal organization requires highly sophisticated empirical theories and skill in modern research methods and analysis, while to manipulate the organizational chart within an unchanging bureaucratic setting does not. Similarly, with all emphasis upon the formal elements, explanations of political phenomena become purely one-dimensional—in the formal organization invariably lies the answer, and the possibility of structure and function being related to operation is ignored.[34] To study the political setting, which the Childs model ignores, requires a keen

33. For example, see Victor Thompson, *Modern Organization* (New York: Alfred A. Knopf, 1961).

34. For example, Childs attributes the demise of the boss' machine to purely formal factors, namely, the short ballot principle as incorporated into the council-manager plan. He does not attribute the eclipse of the machine to such other variables as increased prosperity, the halt of the immigrant influx, the rise of welfare statism and the services it provides (hence, displacing the function often performed by the machine), etc.

In contrast to Childs's simplistic explanation, Robert K. Merton, employing structural-functional analysis, proposed two classifications for variables affecting the status of bossism and the machine. He explains, "To understand the role of bossism and the machine, therefore, we must look at two types of sociological variables: (1) the structural context which makes it difficult, if not impossible, for morally approved structures to fulfill essential social functions, thus leaving the door open for political machines (or their structural equivalents) to fulfill these functions and (2) the subgroups whose distinctive needs are left unsatisfied, except for the latent functions which the machine in fact fulfills." See, "The Functions of the Political Machine," in Sidney Ulmer (ed.), *Introductory Readings in Political Behavior* (Chicago: Rand McNally and Co., 1961), p. 159.

commitment to empirical theory—to ecological and comparative studies—while to manipulate the organizational chart within an unchanging political milieu does not.[35]

This focus upon the formal elements with the consequence of eliminating the demand for causal theory is revealed in other ways. In the models of Gulick and Urwick and Childs, in keeping with their concepts of a rigid hierarchy, "authority" is a matter of firmly ordered levels or grades, and it flows from superior to inferior. Patently, as in the relationship between the manager and council, the emphasis is upon the legal and formal aspects of authority. Other students of administration, accepting the import of the informal organization, have focused attention upon the "area of acceptance"[36] and on "compliance"[37] as vital features of authority. To attempt understanding of these more subtle aspects requires a tough and resilient empirical theory. In the formal

35. The points raised in this paragraph are more applicable to Childs than Weber, for it can be argued that Weber's formal model did fit the German milieu in which it operated.

36. Herbert Simon, *Administrative Behavior* (New York: The Macmillan Co., 1957), p. 133. Simon relied heavily upon Barnard, *Executive.*

37. Amitai Etzioni, *A Comparative Analysis of Complex Organizations* (Glencoe, Illinois: Free Press, 1961). Etzioni writes, "We have chosen the nature of compliance in the organization as a basis for classification. Compliance is a relationship consisting of the power employed by superiors to control subordinates and the orientation of the subordinates to this power. Thus, the study combines a structural and a motivational aspect: structural, since we are concerned with the kinds and distribution of power in organizations; motivational, since we are concerned with the differential commitments of actors to organizations (as units which exercise power over them). . . .

Compliance, we intend to show, is related to many other organizational variables." *Ibid.,* p. xv.

Etzioni develops several different types of models based on varying compliance structures, and he explodes the myth that "organization" is a discrete commodity with unlimited transferability unrelated to differing compliance structures.

models of the classic theorists and Childs such theory is not required.

To Childs, as a traditional organizational theorist, the decision-making process is a simple, rational, and orderly affair. For example, Childs has described the decision-making role of the council as follows, "Allow all your elective officials to come together on an equal footing as a single body, thresh out their differences in debate, and then end them all by the simple expedient of taking a vote, whereupon arguments cease and action begins."[38] To more recent students, the decision-making process is an infinitely more complex and baffling phenomenon[39] and requires a mature empirical theory to understand it. The Childs schema has no such requirement.

Likewise no such theory is needed by the traditionalist in his quest for that prized element of Progressivism and Taylorism—"efficiency." Efficiency per se is a precise and demonstrable fact that can be neatly extricated from its political or administrative setting. As Luther Gulick, one of the principal exponents of traditional organization theory, stated it, "All value scales are environmental with the exception of one—efficiency."[40] Subsequent observers have

38. Richard S. Childs, "How to Work for Charter Reform," *American City*, VIII (February, 1913), 150.
39. For example, see James G. March and Herbert A. Simon, *Organizations* (New York: John Wiley and Sons, Inc., 1958), particularly Chapters 3 and 4; and, Simon, *Administrative Behavior*.
40. Gulick and Urwick (eds.), *Papers on the Science of Administration*, p. 193. Particularly through their association in the Institute of Public Administration, Childs and Gulick have been long-time friends. Childs states that though their personal relationship is a warm and close one, neither man has had any great philosophical impact upon the other. Childs states that this absence of philosophical interaction stems to a large extent from the fact they are in dissimilar fields with Childs being concerned with the "democratic process," and Gulick with "internal government." Interview with the author, January, 1964. My

taken a less simplistic view of the meaning of "efficiency." For example, Dwight Waldo asks, "Efficiency for what? Is not efficiency for efficiency's sake meaningless? *Is efficiency not necessarily measured in terms of other values?* . . . Efficiency cannot itself be a value. Rather, it operates in the interstices of a value system."[41] By the latter conception efficiency becomes related to such matters as "purpose" and "program" and ceases to be simply a matter of maximizing output with limited resources. Rather it seems to relate to the extent to which particular program goals are achieved or not achieved. As a consequence, strong empirical research in the field is needed to attempt to discover precisely what these goals or programs are and to develop valid comparative "measures" of attainment, and to bring even a modicum of understanding of what this deceptive concept means. In contrast, Childs and other traditionalists, in their simplistic view of efficiency, make no similar demand.

Within the context of his organizational theory, Childs, in harmony with traditional attitudes, perceives "leadership" as primarily a matter of universal traits. "Leadership" is not assessed and measured in terms of milieu, situation, or roles. Rather the effective "leader" manifests certain approved traits, while the ineffectual one is lacking them. A recent student has labeled this "the fungibility theory of leadership."[42] Childs has recommended for a city

efforts to elicit comment from Gulick concerning the relationship have been unsuccessful.

41. Dwight Waldo, *The Administrative State* (New York: Ronald Press Co., 1948), p. 202. Also see Robert A. Dahl, "The Science of Public Administration: Three Problems," *Public Administration Review*, VII (Winter, 1947), 2.

42. Robert T. Golembiewski, *Behavior and Organization: O. & M. and the Small Group* (Chicago: Rand McNally and Co., 1962), p. 103.

manager the following traits: "dedication," "cali-
ber," "adaptability," "receptiveness," and "warm-
heartedness."[43] To enumerate traits does not require
a mature causal theory. To explain "leadership" in
terms of "the situation" and of role assignments,
expectations, and attributes requires sophisticated
ecological and comparative studies. It necessitates
sound empirical theory.

Superficially it might appear that in the "principles approach" Childs and the traditionalists have
utilized a strong empirical theory. It is true that the
scientific management school stressed "scientific
method" and "facts" in the construction of a given
"principle"—the "one-best way." Yet, in reality this
approach was often more a priori and normative than
scientific or maturely empirical in its foundation.[44]
More significantly, once a principle was established
normatively with all of its universality and immutabil-
ity, whatever need may have existed for causal
theory ceased. Because the principle was "universal"
in application, no demand was posited by the theory
itself for ecological and comparative studies, and,
since it was immutable like the Newtonian cosmology
and its law of gravity, there was no requirement for
a theory that would allow and facilitate subsequent
testing. In contrast, for those who contend that
"principles" are merely guidelines at best, insepara-

43. Richard S. Childs, "The Enduring Qualities of a Successful
Manager," *Public Management*, XXXXV (January, 1963), pp. 2-3.
For other analyses employing the "trait approach" regarding the man-
ager see Clarence E. Ridley and Orlin F. Nolting, *The City-Manager
Profession* (Chicago: University of Chicago Press, 1934), pp. 41-42,
and White, *The City Manager*, p. 143.

44. Childs has related that he has a friend who has referred to him
in moments of levity as the "grand master" of a priori reasoning in
America. Interview with the author, January, 1964.

ble from environment, and developing in response to environment, a solidly developed empirical theory is imperative.[45]

The sharp dichotomy of policy and administration, characteristic of Progressive thought and strongly reflected in the roles assigned by Childs to the manager and the council, is a simplistic perception of the administrative process that does not require testing in field studies of actual operations and actors. The cleavage is sharp, the roles assigned are limited and specific, and, as a consequence, there is a minimum of overlap assumed between policy formation and policy execution. On the other hand, if policy or politics and administration are viewed as a "seamless web of discretion and action," then a vigorous causal theory is imperative to assist in understanding these inseparable elements.[46]

Childs and traditionalist organizational theory view the organization as a matter of formal elements. Organization, as a behavioral system with the focus on the dynamics and continuous processes of change, is virtually ignored. Partially because of this point of view, Childs lacks any theory of empirical testing, and, as a result, his system is a closed one.

Childs and the Rational Voter

Present in Childs's thought is the belief in a rational voter. In view of his highly rationalistic model that is designed to reflect the "will of the people," it

45. For example, see Dahl, "The Science of Public Administration: Three Problems," *Public Administration Review*, p. 8. John Gaus was the first student to introduce the importance of ecology into the study of public administration. See John M. Gaus, *Reflections on Public Administration* (University, Alabama: University of Alabama Press, 1947).

46. For example, see Waldo, *The Administrative State*.

is probably not astonishing that the voter is expected to act rationally also. In *Short Ballot Principles* Childs has indicated that even if the people voted contrary to his values in a given matter, he would resolutely stand by his democratic commitments and faith in his mechanism of government.[47] Childs's devotion to democratic principles is beyond question, but it can be argued that he has covered his bet for the long pull with an intelligent, educated, and rational voter. His concluding paragraph to *Civic Victories* is revealing: "In all this the objective is simplification, in confidence that when the *most intelligent, best-educated electorate* in the world is thus provided with a sound mechanism for its democratic processes . . . it will, in *visible self-interest*, find its own way out from subjection to self-serving, self-annointed political cliques.

"By that route our children may be free!"[48]

This conception of the rational electorate is closely related to Childs's attitudes analyzed in the two previous sections. In his belief that the group struggle

47. Childs, *Short Ballot Principles* (Boston: Houghton Mifflin Co., 1911), pp. 64, 108. See also Richard S. Childs, "How the Commission-Manager Plan Is Getting Along," *National Municipal Review*, VI (January, 1917), 73.

48. Childs, *Civic Victories*, p. 279. (Italics mine.) Also reflected in this statement is the notion of the Protestant middle-class ethos of who constitutes or should constitute the electorate. This notion is contrary to fact in most large cities. Increasingly today, the central cores of most metropolitan areas are not composed of an "intelligent" and "educated" electorate that perceives its "visible self-interest." Rather this electorate is often developed from the influx of uneducated rural masses, including Southern Negroes, who have been pushed off the land and into the slums of the central areas of the cities. For example, the 1960 census reveals the percentage of Negroes in the following cities, which are among the largest twenty-five in the nation, to be: Atlanta–38.3 per cent, Baltimore–34.8 percent, Chicago–22.9 percent, Cleveland–28.6 per cent, Dallas–19.0 per cent, Detroit–28.9 per cent, Houston–22.9 per cent, Memphis–37.0 per cent, New Orleans–37.2 per cent, New York–14.0 per cent, Philadelphia–26.4 per cent, and St. Louis–28.6 per cent.

will cease with the installation of the proper governmental machine model and that a conflict-free state of equilibrium will ensue, Childs is implicitly placing his faith in an intelligent, educated, rational voter. That is, with the appropriate mechanism reasonable men will perceive their "visible self-interest" *in unison,* and group conflict will ebb away.

Similarly, within his logical, rational, and formal organizational theory Childs visualizes the participant, in this case the voter, in the administrative process as a rational, amenable individual who will play his prescribed role within the formal organization and who will not rebel for irrational, or even nonrational, motives.

In this conception of the voter, as Chapter II indicated, Childs is reflecting general Progressive sentiment. As Gabriel has summed it up, "The Progressive trusted the 'average man' as a voter to use his ballot with intelligence."[49] The impact of this attitude is to make causal theory unnecessary in Childs's scheme as far as consideration of voter behavior. What need is there to test an organism that invariably acts rationally?

In contrast, students of politics in the tradition of Bentley do not perceive a rational voter participating according to his assigned role in a highly formalized administrative and political setting, but rather suspect

49. Ralph H. Gabriel, *The Course of American Democratic Thought* (2d ed.; New York: Ronald Press Co., 1956), p. 362. Progressivism, of course, is merely reflecting the classical democratic theory of the rational citizen found in varying degrees in Locke, Rousseau, Bentham, Paine, and the Founding Fathers generally. Childs could well have uttered Paine's pronouncement that he was "unconnected with any party, and under no sort of influence, public, private, but the influence of reason and principle." M. D. Conway (ed.), *The Writings of Thomas Paine* (New York: G. P. Putnam's Sons, 1894), I, 68.

that the voters' participation in the political process is an infinitely complex phenomenon. They seek to understand this behavior through an increasingly maturing causal theory.[50] The findings of these studies tend to undermine certain tenets of classical democratic thought, particularly the concept of the rational voter.[51] For example, the findings of *The American Voter* suggest there may not be a rational voter of the type presented in Childs's scheme. Campbell and his associates often found the voter as one who lacks interest and information concerning the election and as one who frequently does not approach the electoral process in a mood of reflective study of "the issues."[52]

Levin, in his study *The Alienated Voter*, gives a further illustration of how more recent empirical studies are casting doubt on the classical (and Childs) conception of the rational voter. Levin found in Boston (and he indicates that the situation may be the same in New York City and Philadelphia) "the alienated voter who feels that he is a political outsider—without influence, without power, and without hope."[53] Levin adduces various causal factors producing this alienation, but the significant one for present discussion is the concept itself of the rational voter. The point is made by Levin with this observation:

50. For example, see Stuart A. Rice, *Quantitative Methods in Politics* (New York: Alfred A. Knopf, 1928); P. F. Lazarsfeld *et al.*, *The People's Choice* (2d ed.; New York: Columbia University Press, 1948); B. R. Berelson *et al.*, *Voting* (Chicago: University of Chicago Press, 1954); Angus Campbell *et al.*, *The American Voter* (New York: Wiley, 1960); and Murray B. Levin, *The Alienated Voter* (New York: Holt, Rinehart and Winston, Inc., 1960).

51. For a trenchant analysis, see Eugene Burdick and Arthur J. Brodbeck (eds.), *American Voting Behavior* (Glencoe, Illinois: Free Press, 1959), pp. 136-50.

52. Campbell *et al.*, *The American Voter*, See particularly pages 216-65.

53. Levin, *The Alienated Voter*, p. vii.

". . . city hall is sometimes cleaned up and the average voter continues to feel that he is the political outsider. This is partly because he continues to believe in the classical theory of democracy which leads him to expect more from the political system than is possible."[54] Continuing, Levin writes, "the classical theory of democracy must be revised to fit the realities of modern politics. . . . If individuals continue to believe in the classical view, they will feel politically alienated."[55] In concusion Levin states, "We suggest that a more realistic theory must start from the fact that the masses do not and cannot play the active role, and that elections seldom reveal the 'will' of the majority."[56] The startling implication of *The Alienated Voter* is that not only does the concept of the rational voter not accord with the political realities, but, in addition, the concept—by producing alienated voters whose political expectations are unjustifiably high—is self-defeating, for the voter who believes "that he is not a part of the political process"[57] can hardly be expected to act in a fashion befitting the rational voter of the Childs and classical models.

It is the thesis of this section on "The Closed System" that a utopian philosophical system will remain substantially impervious to change unless accompanied by meaningful empirical theory, which will indicate the need for adjustment of the model to fit the varied and unfolding political, social, and economic realities. Submitted as a corollary thesis is the contention that there is an absence of such theory in

54. *Ibid.,* p. 72.
55. *Ibid.,* p. 74.
56. *Ibid.,* p. 75.
57. *Ibid.,* p. 61.

Childs's philosophy because of his static, formalistic, and rationalistic view of the worlds of politics and administration in which there is no requirement for this tool.

With regard to the second thesis, it might be contended that the converse is also true. That is, that Childs views the realms of politics and administration as he does because he has no theory of testing. In short, do we have the old "chicken-egg" problem? Upon closer examination this alternate thesis appears spurious. Causal theory does not fall as manna from the heavens. Rather it is a felt necessity and its development proceeds from that point. It is "felt" because of the nature of the theorist's view of the political universe. When a student views the areas of politics and administration in the delimited way that Childs does, no "felt" necessity arises. In contrast, Bentley's intellectual heirs view these matters in a fashion that compels this development. They see a multiplicity of causes for the phenomena that concern them and the difficulty in identifying the interrelationships among such phenomena. In sum, the natural evolution of a developing empirical theory is from Bentley to Dahl, and not the reverse.

Childs and the Schubert Schema

Glendon Schubert, in his book *The Public Interest: A Critique of the Theory of a Political Concept*,[58] presents a highly useful schema for a critique of the Childs paradigm. Schubert contends, "The concept of the public interest lies at the heart of the democratic

58. (Glencoe, Illinois: Free Press, 1960).

theories of government.''[59] He offers three classifications of the democratic theorists in their pursuit of
the "public interest": the "idealists," the "realists,"
and the "rationalists." In the first of these categories
the public official ascertains the public interest in a
mystical fashion. He is like the Burkean legislator
whose vision rises above the petty group struggle and
who in a sense divines what he believes to be the public
interest. Schubert states that the idealist is, in his
preferences, "propublic," "antiparty," and "anti-
interest group."

The "realists" believe that the public interest will
arise as a consequence of the group struggle. Arthur
Bentley, David Truman, and their intellectual heirs
reflect this position.[60] Schubert finds the realist is
"propublic," "proparty," and "prointerest group."
Out of the group and party conflict will emerge the
public interest.

To achieve the public interest the "rationalist" contends that the prime problem of administration is to
give effect to the "will of the people." To accomplish
this end Schubert writes, "The model constructed by
the Rationalists is a sausage machine: the public will
is poured into one end and out of the other end drops
neat little segments of the public interest, each
wrapped in its own natural casing."[61] Therefore, it
is in the public interest to rationalize governmental
decision-making, and the governmental apparatus becomes a conduit through which the public will finds
expression, and *ipso facto* the public interest is served.
The rationalists are "propublic," "proparty," and

59. *Ibid.*, p. 4.
60. See Bentley, *The Process of Government*, and David B. Truman,
The Governmental Process (New York: Alfred A. Knopf, 1951).
61. Schubert, *The Public Interest*, p. 221.

"anti-interest group." The proponents of the doctrine of responsible-party government are illustrative of this classification.[62]

Richard Childs furnishes a striking example of the rationalist type. His approach is to construct a system along fairly rigid mechanical lines, and when the "machine" or structure is placed in operation, it is assumed that the "public interest" will emerge. Childs's "concept of democratics" fits squarely within the rationalist classification.

His Three Rules, and all of the various devices expounded by him, serve a distinct function in the construction of his highly rationalistic system. This statement applies to the council-manager plan, nonpartisan elections, elections at large, the short ballot, proportional representation, and other structural concepts with which he deals. Each device is considered essential to the others and to the total framework of his model, out of which is to come the "public interest." Furthermore, Childs rejects any political institution that is dysfunctional to the smooth operation of his rationalistic system. For example, as discussed, he rejects the concept of separation of powers, and, at the municipal level, for the most part, he is antipolitical party. To him both concepts represent loose ends in a nonrational, ill-conceived "machine model."

The Childs system fits the concept that the apparatus of government is a conduit for expression of the "will of the people." The selection of the council and its operation are designed to mirror perfectly the public will. From that point the city manager, as

62. See, for example, American Political Science Association, "Toward a More Responsible Two-Party System," *American Political Science Review* (Supplement), XXXXIV (September, 1950).

administrator, serves as executor of the people's will as reflected in the decisions of the council.

Clearly Childs accepts the "propublic" and "anti-interest group" affinities of the rationalists. As to the first point his entire system is designed to serve the public—in theory it is unquestionably democratic and in keeping with Progressive endeavors to secure such ends. Childs rejects the realist's proposition that out of the group struggle will come the public interest. First of all, as indicated, Childs does not perceive the political process as being basically one of the group conflict. Secondly, a properly constructed scheme will eliminate group conflict in its most virulent form, and if it does persist (it can usually be traced to the machinations of "politicians"), it is an impediment to the machine's maximum proficiency. In any case, in the Childs schema the group struggle is not productive of the public interest.

As to whether Childs conforms to the rationalist's "proparty" attitude, the answer is—it depends. Certainly he rejects out of hand the boss and his machine, for this is the political party run amuck. Undoubtedly most rationalists would agree with him. On that point there seems to be no deviation. As indicated, at the state and national levels Childs accepts the need for parties because of the problem of unwieldy constituencies. Furthermore, as noted, he accepts, in effect, the doctrine of responsible-party government. In this regard he is in harmony with the "proparty" stance of the rationalist. It is at the local level that Childs tends to shift to his "antiparty" position. It is true that he accepts "local parties" in municipal politics, but he accepts them only on a limited basis, and these parties are stunted in their growth compared, for example, with the developed British party system, which Childs greatly admires at the national level. There are "proparty" rationalists (Schattschneiderites) at the local level,[63] but Childs could not be counted among them, for he accepts the local party only as a minor adjunct or supplement to his total model of municipal government.

At times Childs gives evidence of being an "idealist," but in the final analysis this leaning would seem to be more a matter of appearance than reality. At first blush Childs often sounds Burkean (and thus "idealist") in his conception of the council. For example, as the previous chapter related, he argues that once elected the councilmen should be "free agents" obligated to no "political headquarters." However, the vital word is "political." Childs means the individual commissioner should never be obligated to the politicos and their "machines"; he does not mean that the councilman would be deaf to the "will of the people," for if that occurred, then the mechanism would have ceased to produce "democracy" and, consequently, to serve the "public interest."

Similarly, Childs in the ambivalent role he assigns to the manager gives glimpses of Schubert's "idealism." He has indicated that the manager must be a good and virtuous man of exceptional talents and "breadth of vision,"[64] who will render "community leadership." The question arises that if the manager

63. For example, see Gladys M. Kammerer, Charles D. Farris, John M. DeGrove, and Alfred B. Clubok, *City Managers in Politics* (Gainesville, Florida: University of Florida Press, 1962), p. 89; and, Marvin A. Harder, *Nonpartisan Elections: A Political Illusion?* (New York: Holt, 1958), p. 15.

64. For example, see Richard S. Childs, "The Enduring Qualities of a Successful Manager," *Public Management*, XXXXV (January, 1963), 2-4.

is primarily an "expert" and "conduit," one of the roles which Childs assigns, why demand of him such extraordinary talents? Is it because as an "idealist" administrator he is to "divine" the public interest through his own "small voice of conscience"? The temptation is to answer affirmatively, and to a limited extent that would be true. However, beneath this appearance of "idealism" Childs still remains basically a "rationalist." The purpose in demanding such impressive abilities of the manager is not to insure that he will be equipped to divine the public interest through examination of his own conscience, but rather, so that he will be a sufficiently wise and perceptive person to enable him to sense the *public* will, and then to undertake policy initiation. He will serve as a pump primer in getting the mechanism into operation. At least in theory Childs remains loyal to his rationalistic scheme—even with his manager providing "community leadership." In Childs's philosophy all avenues ultimately lead to his highly rationalistic machine model and to the closed system that encompasses it. It is with the effect of this closed system that the ensuing chapter is concerned.

V

Critique of the Model:
The Effect
of the Closed System

"As a nation we have never been more than merely superficial in our theories of political science." Richard S. Childs, 1909.[1]

The Effect on Methodology

When a philosophical system closes for want of causal theory, profound results ensue. Appropriate as a point of departure is to consider the impact upon Childs's methodology for testing his model in operation. The inference from the preceding chapter might be that since Childs has no empirical theory, likewise he has no methodology. However, this is not actually the case. There is no doubt that Childs lacks a genuine

1. Richard S. Childs, *Short Ballot Principles* (Boston: Houghton Mifflin Co., 1911), p. 1.

causal theory, but it does not follow that there is a total absence of methodology. The latter element is present, but because empirical theory is absent, it appears in an underdeveloped and basically unreliable form.

This latter point is poignantly illustrated in the fact that Childs on one occasion can speak of his paradigm as "based on scientifically sound action,"[2] while on another he can refer to his "fond *a priori* theories."[3] It would appear on the surface that this presents an irreconcilable inconsistency. That is, either something is rooted in a tough-minded scientific method or it is a priori, but it cannot be both at the same time. But in Childs's thought there is no genuine conflict because his "scientific" method is at such a rudimentary level of development that the difference between it and a priori rationalism is negligible. This stunted development of methodology results from the absence of causal theory, for where the latter does not exist there is no opportunity or reason for the former to grow.

Illustrative of this low level of development is Childs's acceptance of the Stone, Price, and Stone study, *City Manager Government in the United States: A Review after Twenty-Five Years,*[4] as incontestable evidence of the superiority of the city-manager form of government. In fact, Childs concludes, "The burden of proof is henceforth all on the opposition to the

2. Richard S. Childs, "League's Second Stretch," *National Municipal Review,* XXXIII (November, 1944), 519.

3. Richard S. Childs, "The City Manager Plan Passes Its 'Exams,'" *National Municipal Review,* XXIX (July, 1940), 444.

4. (Chicago: Public Administration Service, 1940). See also by the same authors, *City Manager Government in Nine Cities* (Chicago: Public Administration Service, 1940).

[council-manager] movement.''[5] The Stone, Price, and Stone studies do have their virtues and methodologically they represent an auspicious start, but if they are offered as the final proof of the pre-eminence of the manager form then, in Herson's words, "the bareness of the evidentiary cupboard stands revealed.''[6]

A further example of Childs's simplistic methodology is his contention, "The fact that 74 per cent of city managers are chosen from out of town has become one of the proofs of the nonpolitical character of these governments. . . .''[7] It might well be contended that this is not only weak empirical method, but in fact, questionable logic. Even using "political" in the restrictive sense that Childs does, it by no means follows that because the manager is selected from outside the community that this is "proof" of the "nonpolitical character" of the manager plan. His initial selection may have stemmed from political turmoil within the community (perhaps his predecessor, "a local boy," was fired because of his local status, as, for example, would be the case in the dominance of a faction dedicated to a "professional," and, therefore, an outsider), or the manager may subsequently be drawn (willing or not) into the political

5. Richard S. Childs, ''The City Manager Plan Passes Its 'Exams,' '' *National Municipal Review*, p. 447. See also Childs, ''League's Second Stretch,'' *National Municipal Review*, p. 518; and, Richard S. Childs, ''The City Manager Plan Will Endure,'' *American City*, LV (May, 1940), 36.

6. Lawrence J. R. Herson, ''The Lost World of Municipal Government,'' *American Political Science Review*, LI (June, 1957), 341.

7. Richard S. Childs, *Civic Victories: The Story of an Unfinished Revolution* (New York: Harper and Brothers, 1952), p. 166. See also Richard S. Childs, ''Quest for Leadership,'' *National Civic Review*, L (November, 1961), 529; and, Richard S. Childs, ''Council-Manager Cities 1,000 Strong,'' *American City*, LXVI (January, 1951), 70.

orbit. In sum, the fact that the manager is selected from without may be proof of something, but it is not proof of the absence of "politics" in council-manager government.

Another example of the underdeveloped status of Childs's method is found in a survey conducted in 1949 by the National Municipal League in forty-eight cities to determine whether nonpartisan elections had operated according to the model. A questionnaire was directed to newspapers, chambers of commerce, and city managers. The query posed was, "Do Republican or Democratic city committees throw their weight, officially or unofficially, openly or covertly, despite the nonpartisan theory of elections?"[8] Childs relates that the answer was resoundingly and "universally 'no' " with "three partial exceptions," and Childs quickly disposes of these deviant cases. Childs concluded "This testimony . . . demonstrates that politics without politicians is actually with us!"[9] The model was exonerated; however, conducting a public opinion poll with a leading question directed to chambers of commerce and city managers to ascertain the theoretical efficacy of nonpartisan elections is questionable as to methodological soundness.[10] To use Herson's phrase, "the standards of proof" are wanting.[11]

8. Richard S. Childs, " '500 'Non-political' Elections," *National Municipal Review*, XXXVIII (June, 1949), 278.

9. *Ibid.*, p. 282.

10. For evidence of contrary findings where a more advanced methodology was employed see Eugene C. Lee, *The Politics of Nonpartisanship* (Berkeley, California: University of California Press, 1960), pp. 98, 102, and *passim*; and, Oliver P. Williams and Charles R. Adrian, "The Insulation of Local Politics Under the Nonpartisan Ballot," *American Political Science Review*, LII (December, 1959), 1052-63.

11. Herson, "The Lost World of Municipal Government," *American Political Science Review*, p. 338.

The Problem of Inconsistency

In addition to a stunted methodology, part and parcel of the closed system and the absence of causal theory is the fact that ideas do not change over time. In 1963, Childs wrote, "I doubt if by tracing through [my] writings in chronological order you will find that I have changed any of my ideas since 1909. . . ."[12] Early in 1964, Childs recommended that I conclude this study with the statement, "Mr. Childs has started off with a theory fifty years ago and hasn't changed since."[13] My research completely affirms Childs's prediction made in his letter, and it would be appropriate to terminate with his proposed statement.[14]

Though Childs's concepts have not altered over the years, their reception has fluctuated. For example, Don K. Price has postulated that because of the appeal of the council-manager plan to the business world with its corporate organizational form and the emphasis upon economy and efficiency, the plan was probably least popular during the Great Depression when the business image suffered.[15] The statistics on the adoption of the plan tend to support Price's thesis. The *Municipal Yearbook* indicates that between 1934, the first year in which the *Yearbook* was published, and 1940 the percentage increase in adoptions in all cities of over 1,000 population jumped from 6.7 per cent to only 7.1 per cent. Conceivably, as Price has hypothesized, the Depression was having its effect. In contrast, during the prosperous decade of the

12. Letter to the author, October 22, 1963.
13. Interview with the author, January, 1964.
14. The notable exception to this is Childs's shift from commission government to the city manager form discussed in Chapter III.
15. Don K. Price, "The Promotion of the Council-Manager Plan," *Public Opinion Quarterly*, V (1941), 570.

1950's with the middle-class flight to the suburbs, the percentage increase in adoptions in all cities of over 5,000 population jumped from 24.3 per cent in 1950 to 38 per cent in 1960. These figures suggest that the appeal of the plan has been affected by prevailing economic and social conditions.[16]

Where empirical theory is absent and a closed system which remains unchanged through time results, the problem of inconsistency often arises. The model and the ideas upon which it is founded do not change, but it does not follow that the worlds of politics and administration likewise remain unaltered. The end product can be inconsistency.

For example, Childs contends that the foundation of his value system is to construct a governmental mechanism that is highly sensitive and "responsive" to the "will of the people." Within the confines of his model the city-manager form of government fits those requirements perfectly. Where the chance of inconsistency arises is that if it were ever empirically established that Childs's ideal type is not the most "reponsive" form of government for a given political setting, then Childs is confronted with an inconsistency between his professed political values and the realities of the specific situation.

Parenthetically it can be argued that such concepts as "the will of the people" and "responsiveness" are inadequate tools to describe and evaluate the functioning of any political system. As the previous discussion of Childs and the Group Theory of Politics has suggested, Bentley and his intellectual followers have considered such a monolithic concept as "the will of

16. All statistics were obtained from the *Municipal Yearbook* (Chicago: International City Managers' Association, 1934–to date) for the particular year in question.

the people" as out of touch with political reality, for there is in fact no single, identifiable manifestation of a "public will."[17] In addition, the term "responsiveness" is a vague generality that in the final analysis is of slight value in ascertaining the validity of a given form of local government in a particular political environment. It seems more realistic not to state the matter in such imprecise terms, but rather to state the problem in terms of the effectiveness of a particular governmental structure in a given ecological setting to anticipate emerging problems (for example, racial strife, crime, poverty, etc.), and to deal decisively and effectively with them before they reach crisis proportions. Childs might argue that his terminology is merely a shorthand method of saying this same thing. Even if this is the case, the problem of inconsistency persists because Childs has a closed system in which his ideal paradigm remains, for the most part, impervious to testing and adjustment. As a result, there always remains the possibility of inconsistency between the *assumed* effectiveness of his ideal

17. There is growing evidence from recent empirical studies which reveals "city politics" as a matter of great variety, complexity, and flux rather than as any simple case of a monolithic "public will." For example, see Edward C. Banfield, *Political Influence* (Glencoe, Illinois: Free Press, 1961); Edward C. Banfield and Martin M. Meyerson, *Politics, Planning, and the Public Interest* (Glencoe, Illinois: Free Press, 1955); Robert A. Dahl, *Who Governs?* (New Haven: Yale University Press, 1961); Gladys M. Kammerer, Charles D. Farris, John M. DeGrove, and Alfred B. Clubok, *The Urban Political Community* (Boston: Houghton Mifflin Co., 1963); Roscoe C. Martin *et al.*, *Decisions in Syracuse* (Bloomington, Indiana: Indiana University Press, 1961); and James Q. Wilson, *Negro Politics* (Glencoe, Illinois: Free Press, 1960).

The last study is a particularly striking illustration of the point. Wilson finds that Negro groups in Chicago are highly diversified and often at odds in their respective approaches to solving the Negro's problems; consequently, even with this deprived and isolated minority group, where one might most expect to find a single "public will," the realities show remarkably variegated patterns.

model in a given community and its *actual* effectiveness.

Edward Sofen's study of the Dade Metro system is suggestive of how this problem of inconsistency might arise.[18] Sofen postulates that in order to have effective municipal government in a large metropolitan area such as Miami there must be maximum leadership initiative. The inference is strong in his study that he believes the ideal (or Childs) manager plan is not the form best suited for producing the goal of effective government through maximum leadership. Sofen offers the following "evidence."

The Council, which by Childs's theory is supposed to afford the policy-making thrust, is not doing so. First, the manager has a virtual monopoly on the needs and facts of an existing or proposed policy program.[19] Therefore, to expect the council to be the spearhead of policy formulation, as Childs's schema provides, when so dependent on the manager is unrealistic.[20] Secondly, completely out of keeping with the role assigned in the Childs paradigm, Sofen contends that the council instead of consciously providing policy leadership, intentionally avoids it as a political hazard. In fact, the more experienced councilmen become (and, consequently, according to the model the more valuable as policy initiators), the more "they are likely to try to insure their future by avoiding the hazards of political leadership. . . ."[21] With the

18. Edward Sofen, *The Miami Metropolitan Experiment* (Bloomington, Indiana: Indiana University Press, 1963).
19. *Ibid.*, p. 205.
20. *Ibid.*
21. *Ibid.*, p. 206. See also Charles R. Adrian, "A Study of Three Communities," *Public Administration Review*, XVIII (Spring, 1958), 212.

council not providing leadership as prescribed by the model, and with the manager by the model design not supposed to fill the vacuum that results, the question is presented (but by no means resolved)[22] by the Sofen study as to whether the Childs model in a large metropolitan area in reality affords the zenith of effective (or to use Childs's phrase, "responsive") government, as Childs insists that it does. Because he lacks causal theory and presents a sealed system, Childs could well be confronted with an inconsistency between his value system (government that is sensitive to "the will" of the electorate), as incorporated into his model, and the realities of municipal government.[23]

22. Sofen's study is discussed because it offers an empirical introduction to the problem of inconsistency; however, by employing this study I am not suggesting that Sofen has "proven" the inadequacy of manager government in the Dade Metro system. For example, it may be that the "leadership problem" in that system does not stem principally from any inadequacies of the ideal manager plan, but rather, it results from the over-all amorphous and fragmented nature of political life in the Dade County areas, as well as in Florida generally. (On this latter point, see V. O. Key's analysis of Florida politics in *Southern Politics* (New York: Alfred A. Knopf, 1949), Chapter 5, "Florida: Every Man for Himself.") Furthermore, Dade County Metro was established as a federal system to facilitate and "sell" adoption of the plan. This federal system represented a variation from the model plan, and undoubtedly contributes to the political fragmentation (i.e., the "leadership problem") on the council. Thus in reality it may be that this deviation from the model design has produced the alleged leadership gap and not the model itself. The problem of federalism, and the fragmentation it tends to produce, were partially dealt with in the 1963 Dade County Metro charter amendments which provided for at-large elections, along with the popular election of a mayor to preside over the commission.

In sum, Sofen's study is offered for the questions it raises rather than for any it resolves.

23. As explored previously, Childs vehemently rejects the "alternative" proposal in the new draft of the Model City Charter which allows the electorate to select the mayor-commissioner. Interesting is the commentary offered by the League as to why the alternative is allowed: "When problems brought about by economic and social change, in-

This problem of the effectiveness of the mechanism goes to the very heart of Childs's philosophical scheme, and if here he has become entangled in an inconsistency, it is a serious one. Another equally grave inconsistency will result if Childs fails to adjust his model to the political realities that subsequent empirical studies may reveal. Repeatedly Childs, as examined in Chapter III, has proclaimed that the problems of government have to do with the mechanism and not "human nature," for the latter element cannot be changed; therefore, the structure must be designed to accommodate it. Consequently, to maintain consistency, if subsequent testing should reveal that the Childs ideal model is not in keeping with the realities of human behavior, he should adjust his paradigm accordingly. To fail to do so inexorably presents a contradiction between professed value and reality.

---

cluding shifts of population, demand aggressive municipal action to effect solutions, municipal election campaigns frequently turn on specific policy commitments and programs. The forces for particular programs need political spokesmen who will lead the fight for these policies. Although it is not always the case, a candidate running for the office of mayor with a team of council candidates supporting him goes into office with a mandate to pursue particular programs. Alternative Section 2.03 therefore provides for the separately elected mayor." *Model City Charter* (Draft of Commentary) (New York: National Municipal League, 1963), p. 5.

Although he did not recommend it for Miami at that time (1962), Sofen concluded, "The election by the voters of a county commission chairman, under a council-manager form of government, might under some conditions have merit." Sofen, *Miami Experiment*, p. 206.

Others would remedy the "inconsistency" through the general-manager form or the strong-mayor form. For example, see respectively Wallace S. Sayre, "The General Manager Idea for Large Cities," *Public Administration Review*, XIV (Spring, 1954), 253-58; and, S. Freedgood, "New Strength in City Hall," in *The Exploding Metropolis* (Garden City, New York: Doubleday, 1958).

The Ideal Model and Political Reality

The possibility of inconsistency, because of a closed system and absence of causal theory, permeates Childs's entire scheme, and the items discussed in the preceding subsection, though the most fundamental, are only suggestive of the magnitude of this problem. Because various facets of the Childs schema are subject to intense empirical studies, and possible gaps between the ideal model and the political realities may be revealed, the potential of inconsistency will loom larger. No pretense is made that all such studies presently in print have been exhausted in the preparation of this analysis. In fact, for reasons of significance and illustration, principal emphasis will be placed upon the role of the manager in Childs's design. Less extensively, the matters of proportional representation and nonpartisan elections will be considered.

The Role of the Manager

The role of the manager within the formal model has been discussed previously, and need not be repeated at length. A brief résumé will suffice. Childs has written, "The position of city manager, of course, is the central feature of the plan. . . ."[24] Because of the obvious significance of the manager, Childs has written extensively about his position in the schema, and, as suggested, the result has been possible ambivalence or even glaring inconsistency.

On the one hand, rooted in the Progressive concept

24. Richard S. Childs, "How the Commission-Manager Plan Is Getting Along," *National Municipal Review*, IV (July, 1915), 373.

of the separation of policy and administration, Childs expounds, "The idea is that the council is to act always as a whole and stick to policy and that the manager is not to govern but to administer."[25] On the other hand, Childs approvingly writes that "managers are up to their ears in policy-proposing," and he concludes, "As in any private business, the manager has always been entitled to the fullest hearing and chance to lead the council members toward determinations of matters about which he may usually know more than they do. The leadership in policy which city managers are contributing on issues great or routine is not only a sound enrichment of municipal practice but is also in accord with the initial design. Lead on!"[26] In one breath Childs allows that *after* the council has adopted a policy the manager may "promote or defend" it "publicly," yet, in the same article with only one paragraph intervening, he cautions "that the manager should play no part in . . . identifying himself with any of the community's parties or factions."[27]

In the world of "real" politics and administration, these contradictions are probably irreconcilable; however, it may be that within the Childs schema, though there may be ambivalence, there is not a totally inexplicable inconsistency. To seek an explanation it is essential to recall to mind Childs's view of the world of politics and administration and his theories of organization. It will be remembered in the Childs schema that the group conflict and politics and administration, as a *process*, are relegated to peripheral

25. Childs, *Civic Victories*, p. 171.
26. Childs, "Quest for Leadership," *National Civic Review*, pp. 529, 539.
27. Richard S. Childs *et al.*, *Best Practice with the Manager Plan* (New York: National Municipal League, 1963), p. 6.

status. As in the example of Dayton, it is the perfected state of equilibrium—the very absence of process—that is the sought-for ideal. It is within this framework that the manager can be a "policy proposer" and yet at the same time avoid being caught up in the policy-making process (politics in the broad sense), because, ideally, process will be absent. The manager will make proposals (even ones of great vision), which any manager with comparable training and *expertise* might make, and the council, without factions and with all due orderliness and reasoned deliberation, will dispose of the matter.[28] Finally, the rational electorate (from which the manager had probably divined his ideas initially) will acquiesce. In sum, within the Childs schema the manager has proposed policy, it has been acted upon, and it will be administered, and all of this has occurred without the manager being caught up in that processual phenomenon often called "politics."

Similarly, Childs's organization theory, with its emphasis upon the *formal* elements, partially explains what otherwise might be irreconcilable contradiction. Within the Childs design, even though the manager is up to his "ears in policy-proposing," he can avoid the entanglements of conflict and process (if there be any) by close adherence to the prescriptions of the organizational chart.

Early in his career Childs suggested the appropriateness of this approach. In the initial years of the manager movement City Manager R. C. Horne of Beaufort, South Carolina, was dismissed from this position for attempting on his own initiative to enforce

---

28. As hypothesized in the previous discussion of Dayton's politics, the very lack of faction in the council may mean exclusion of significant groups from access to decision making.

a tax ordinance, which had lain dormant for years. Childs relates that Manager Horne launched his crusade with ''a sudden attack upon the leading bank, the president and cashier of which constituted two of his three commissioners, with a policeman, a warrant and a demand for $10,000 of back taxes.''[29] Childs relates, ''Incidentally, of course, he lost his job and was supplanted by another manager of different disposition.''[30]

Childs's advice to former Manager Horne is highly indicative of his stress upon the formal organization and of the necessity of the manager to adhere to the formalities of his role:

I say it was right enough if he felt like doing it, but quite outside of his profession. [If he had been mayor it would have been permissible.] But he was not mayor—he was city manager. He stepped out of his profession. . . . He was frankly insubordinate. He took what was for one in his position a disorderly way to rectify a wrong. The orderly way would have been to present a formal proposal to a public meeting of the commission explaining openly and clearly the situation as he saw it. The commission would have to find an excuse for turning him down and would do so. The manager would then have his personal record clear. Unofficially he could privately call the attention of some of the local citizens to the incident and even wink in doing so, thus being personally disloyal, but not officially disloyal, to the commissioners who have no right to expect him to keep secrets for them . . . at any rate it is, I think, the professional way.[31]

Over thirty years later Childs confirmed his belief that if the manager wished to avoid the pitfalls of

29. Richard S. Childs *et al.*, ''Professional Standards and Professional Ethics in the New Profession of City Manager: A Discussion,'' *National Municipal Review*, V (April, 1916), 199.
30. *Ibid.*
31. *Ibid.*

"leadership in policy" he ought to remain close to the outlines of the formal organization. With simplistic faith he has written, "City managers must, of course, frequently defend their decisions or purposes in technical matters, but the *perfect* protection of the manager lies . . . in his ability to say to an irate constituent: 'Those men you voted for for the council have looked into this and agree that it is all right.' "[32]

It may be then that within the confines of Childs's philosophy there is no inconsistency between what appear to be conflicting roles assigned to the manager.[33] Still the stubborn problem remains regarding these roles as to whether there is in fact a gap between the ideal model and the "real world" of municipal government. Built upon the conception of politics as process, and, consequently, employing causal theory, there are empirical studies suggesting that a gap does exist. The most intensive study, conducted by Gladys M. Kammerer and her associates at the University of Florida, relates to "an analysis of manager tenure and termination."[34] The authors write, "We originally conceived of this study as an attempt to explain the rather short tenure of Florida city managers during the postwar period."[35] By framing hypothe-

32. Richard S. Childs, "Theories of Responsive Government Prove Practical," *Public Management*, XXIX (December, 1947), 356. (Italics mine.)

33. Childs is by no means unique in his ambivalence on the manager's role. For example, the International City Managers' Association reflects the same position. See *The City Manager's Code of Ethics* (Chicago: International City Managers' Association, 1963), and Clarence E. Ridley, *The Role of the City Manager in Policy Formulation* (Chicago: International City Managers' Association, 1958), pp. 18, 21, 47.

34. Gladys M. Kammerer, Charles D. Farris, John M. DeGrove, and Alfred B. Clubok, *City Managers in Politics* (Gainesville, Florida: University of Florida Press, 1962).

35. *Ibid.*, p. 1.

ses, and carrying on extensive field research in collecting empirical data, the authors tested several variables and their impact upon the central problem of manager tenure and termination. It is important to observe that the team viewed " 'politics' as the *process* of making 'significant,' sanctioned, community-wide decisions.' "[36] They conceived the political world in the tradition of Bentley rather than in that of Childs.

As to their findings the authors write: "The causal nexus that our study has uncovered seems, to us, fairly clear. Of the several classes of independent variables that we hypothesized as explanations of the varying lengths and the terminations of manager appointments, *the most important seem to be the political factors:* political style or type of politics (monopoly—oligopoly—competition), the occurrence of power exchanges (or power plays), and the consequent level of political stability in the towns."[37] Continuing, the team found: "Managers tend to play policy roles in the making of the principal decisions of the city, and, therefore, they tend to incur political hazards.—We found no managers in our case-study cities who were not involved in the making, shaping, or vetoing of policy proposals. Therefore, they were right in the heart of politics, in the broadest sense of that term, to the extent that certain interests might well be alienated as a result of actions taken by the council on manager recommendations. Such alienated persons might and sometimes did seek political retaliation. The manager is an expedient focus for retaliation."[38] Finally, the authors conclude, "City

36. *Ibid.,* p. 11. (Italics mine.)
37. *Ibid.,* p. 72. (Italics mine.)
38. *Ibid.,* p. 83.

managers we found were in politics *ipso facto* by the
very nature of their jobs."[39]

Ralph A. Straetz, in his study *PR Politics in
Cincinnati*,[40] tends to corroborate those findings.
Straetz too perceives the world of politics as a processual phenomenon, and he finds that the manager in
Cincinnati has been inexorably pulled into the politics
of that city. Straetz writes, "Both the use of a city
manager and the city manager himself have been an
intermittent issue in Queen City campaigns over the
past thirty years."[41]

Straetz further finds that the major participants in
the political struggles of Cincinnati "recognize that
administration is an extension of politics and policy
making, and so the controversy over the manager
revolves around the role of that official in the making
of policy as well as the carrying out of his administrative responsibilities."[42] Thus Straetz finds that the
manager is not only involved in "politics," but, in
addition, his conclusions tend to undermine that
doctrinal tenet of the Childs schema which accepts a
fairly rigid dichotomy of policy and administration.[43]
He deduces on the basis of his evidence that "policy
making and administration cannot be completely
separated."[44]

The Florida team of political scientists and
Straetz believe that they have found an incongruity

39. *Ibid.*, p. 86.
40. (New York: New York University Press, 1958.)
41. *Ibid.*, p. 253.
42. *Ibid.*, p. 267.
43. There is a recent piece of evidence indicating that Childs may
be altering his doctrinal position on this matter. In 1963 he wrote,
"Strictly speaking, there can be no complete separation of policy and
administration. A rough understanding of the dividing line is generally worked out in experience." Childs *et al., Best Practice*, p. 4.
44. Straetz, *PR Politics in Cincinnati*, p. 268.

between the Childs ideal model and the "realities" of municipal government. In effect, they conclude that Childs's ambivalence on the manager's role is an irreconcilable inconsistency. They conclude that the manager is ineluctably caught up in a process they choose to call "politics."[45]

This conflict over the position of the manager between the newer empirical studies and Childs's model is symptomatic of a basic conflict over the problem of "role." Straetz's study brings this matter into focus. Not only did Straetz find in Cincinnati that the manager is involved in the political process, but he found that the stanchest supporters of the manager plan expect the manager to play a political role. He relates, "Charter's attitude has not been nonpartisan. Rather it has desired managers who share its interests and concern for social problems and municipal reform. . . ."[46]

45. Among other reasons, these two studies were selected for analysis because of their strong empirical base. There are numerous articles, more insightful than empirical, suggesting that the manager is a political animal. For example, see Karl A. Bosworth, "The Manager *Is* a Politician," *Public Administration Review*, XVIII (Winter, 1958), 216-22; Gladys M. Kammerer, "Is the Manager a Political Leader?—Yes," *Public Management*, XXXXIV (February, 1962), 26-29; Don K. Price, "The Promotion of the Council-Manager Plan," *Public Opinion Quarterly*, V (1941), 573; John M. Pfiffner, "Policy Leadership—For What?" *Public Administration Review*, XIX (Winter, 1959), 121-24; and, James Q. Wilson, "Manager Under Fire," in Richard T. Frost (ed.), *Cases in State and Local Government* (Englewood Cliffs, New Jersey: Prentice-Hall, 1961), pp. 17-27.

Though Childs did not accept it as such, the Stone, Price, and Stone study, on which he relied as conclusive proof of the superiority of the manager form, is highly suggestive of the fact that the manager is a participant, willing or not, in a political world of *process*. The three classifications ("machine cities," "faction-ridden cities," and "community-governed cities") are, in effect, predicated upon this proposition. See Harold A. Stone, Don K. Price, and Kathryn H. Stone, *City Manager Government in the United States: A Review after Twenty-Five Years* (Chicago: Public Administration Service, 1940).

46. Straetz, *PR Politics in Cincinnati*, p. 253.

Eulau has written, "... role seems to commend itself as a basic unit of social and political analysis."[47] Straetz's finding corroborates this view: it suggests that role analysis is a tool of great potential in studying the manager's participation in the political process. For example, the Childs model assumes a role consensus regarding the manager's functions and disregards the possibilities of role conflict. By not perceiving the dynamics of competing groups, Childs conceives all participants in municipal government as viewing the manager's role as purely one of administration and *expertise*. As Straetz's finding would suggest, many groups (consciously or unconsciously) may view the manager as serving in a political role, and their expectations are governed accordingly. The inevitable result is a conditioning of the manager's behavior to accommodate those expectations.

Aside from group expectations, there may be other variables affecting the manager's behavior. In this regard, the application of role analysis remains virtually untapped. Gladys M. Kammerer has made an auspicious start in her consideration of an institutional-structural variable.[48] Professor Kammerer was concerned with the impact of the popular election of the mayor (in violation of Childs's doctrine) upon the role of the manager. She concludes: "One may justly conclude that if the political end sought in a particular community is to enhance popular control and reduce authority of an appointed administrator, or at least to frustrate that appointed administrator, then the structural arrangement to accomplish this in council-

47. Heinz Eulau, *The Behavioral Persuasion in Politics* (New York: Random House, 1963), p. 40.

48. Gladys M. Kammerer, "Role Diversity of City Managers," *Administrative Science Quarterly*, VIII (March, 1964), 421-22.

manager government is to elect the mayor by popular vote."[49]

Role analysis is an incisive tool in analyzing not only the position of the manager but in studying all the basic components of the Childs schema. As previously indicated, Childs, in constructing his ideal type, assigned formal roles to the principal components of his paradigm: the manager, the council, the press, and the voters. In determining whether any incongruities exist between these formal roles and political reality, role analysis should be extremely useful. Instructive is the study by Neal Gross and his associates who analyzed the operation of the school board and the relationships between the board and the superintendent within a role analysis framework.[50] For example, the authors hypothesized, empirically tested, and found "that school board members and superintendents, in defining the division of responsibilities between their positions, would each assign greater responsibility than the other to his own position."[51] It has been noted that Childs considered the school-board–superintendent structure as mechanically perfect, and, furthermore, he employed this model in the building of his council-manager plan. Therefore, Gross's study is particularly suggestive of the potential that role analysis offers in the study of Childs's model and in ascertaining the extent to which it varies from political reality. In the Childs schema, "role" is a simplistic notion of formal assignment, and each component is delegated basically *one* role as seen in

49. *Ibid.*, p. 442.
50. Neal Gross *et al.*, *Explorations in Role Analysis: Studies of the School Superintendency Role* (New York: John Wiley and Sons, Inc., 1958).
51. *Ibid.*, p. 30.

the manager's position as "administrator" and the council's function as "policy maker." In contrast, more recent researchers employing role analysis, such as Kammerer and Gross, suggest that the matter is more realistically one of *roles* with all of the richness, variety, and diversity that a pluralistic conception of role presents.

Proportional Representation

Straetz, in his conclusions on the role played by proportional representation in Cincinnati, adduces further evidence that there may be a gap between Childs's model and political reality. In Chapter II it was noted that "P. R." was a cog designed to promote the "smooth running" of Childs's machine model. Childs was impressed with its "mathematical precision," and he argued that it assisted in taking "the chess play out of politics."[52] This device was particularly necessary, Childs contended, in order to assure compliance with Rule Two (wieldy constituencies), for in large electoral districts it enabled the individual candidate to seek election without the aid of political parties. This was the doctrinal rationale.

The empirical data presented by Straetz suggests that the effect of "P. R." has been precisely the opposite of that intended. Instead of promoting harmony and a friction-free mechanism by including on the council all elements of the community, Straetz finds, "P. R. elections have on the whole been hard fought and close, with specific alternatives proposed to the public. And this characteristic has existed in Cincinnati in this century only during the life of P. R."[53]

52. Childs, *Civic Victories*, pp. 163, 248-49.
53. Straetz, *PR Politics in Cincinnati*, p. 268.

In lieu of producing a tranquil state of equilibrium, proportional representation has accentuated the group struggle.[54] Similarly, instead of eliminating the need for parties as doctrine provided, Straetz found that the effect of P. R. was precisely the reverse. He writes, "For thirty years it has provided a workable and effective two-party system in one of the largest cities in the country."[55]

Nonpartisan Elections

As regards nonpartisan elections, there also may be a disparity between Childs's doctrine and actuality. At least those who view "process" as the substance of politics are producing suggestive findings. As will be recalled from Chapter III, within Childs's schema the purpose of the nonpartisan election was to drive the national political parties from the local scene by prohibiting the appearance of party labels on the municipal ballot. Both traditionalists, like Childs, and those of the "behavioral persuasion," like Eugene Lee and Charles Adrian, can agree that this legal requirement has impaired the formal operation of the national parties. Lee, in his study of nonpartisanship in six California cities, found that *"formal* activity by the two party organizations is relatively infrequent in local politics,"[56] while Adrian has concluded, "With

54. Charles P. Taft's study of Cincinnati confirms this. See Charles P. Taft, *City Management: The Cincinnati Experiment* (New York: Farrar and Rinehart, 1933), p. 94. Price has stated that this effect of P. R. was inevitable. See Price, "The Promotion of the City Manager Plan," p. 576.

55. Because P. R. has facilitated and promoted the group struggle and political party competition, Straetz regrets that it was abolished in Cincinnati. (Like Schubert's "rationalist" he believes that out of these conflicts will come the "public interest.") Therefore, he approves of this device, according to the doctrine, for precisely the wrong reasons.

56. Lee, *The Politics of Nonpartisanship*, p. 117. (Italics mine.)

few exceptions, nonpartisan elections have . . . effectively removed the *regular party machinery* from involvement in . . . local . . . elections."[57] Childs, as a result of his test of nonpartisan elections (discussed in a previous section of this chapter as a problem in methodology), would agree with these findings.[58]

Where the conflict arises is whether there is "informal" activity by the party organizations. Childs with his preoccupation with the formal elements of organization, coupled with a methodology unadapted to probing into the informal processes, concludes, in effect, that since there is no formal activity there is *ipso facto* no informal interference either.[59] Childs is satisfied that the world of municipal government has been safely insulated from national partisan activity, be it of a formal or informal variety.

In contrast, empirical studies by Lee and Adrian intimate that the question of informal interference is a cloudy one. In summing up the findings in his six California cities, Lee states, "Partisanship (the impact of the two major parties) ranged from nonexistence in Maywood to the strongly partisan situation in Berkeley where at times, as one observer noted, everything bore the party label *except* the ballot.''[60] Though party names did not appear on the ballot, Berkeley

57. Charles R. Adrian, "A Typology for Nonpartisan Elections," *Western Political Quarterly*, XII (June, 1959), 456. (Italics mine.)
58. Childs, "500 'Non-Political' Elections," *National Municipal Review*, pp. 278-82.
59. It is true that Childs in his questionnaire appeared to be searching for informal meddling with the query, "Do Republican or Democratic city committees throw their weight, officially or unofficially, openly or covertly . . . ?" *Ibid.*, p. 278. However, as the previous discussion on methodology has suggested, Childs may appear to be exploring the informal process, but whether in fact he is doing so is questionable.
60. Lee, *The Politics of Nonpartisanship*, p. 98.

was characterized by "hotly contested and partisan-structured contests."[61]

Adrian and Williams also present evidence suggesting that the influence of the national parties is present in the local setting. In a 1959 study of four Michigan cities correlations were found between municipal nonpartisan slate voting and state and national party voting.[62] Furthermore, it was found that the correlation increased with the intensification of issue politics. The inescapable inference is that, as a matter of informal processes, the nonpartisan election is not as free of national partisan influence as Childs's doctrine prescribes or believes exists. As Lee phrases the question, "How partisan are nonpartisan politics?"[63]

A further incongruity, attributable to nonpartisanship, may be found between the ideal paradigm and actuality. Whatever Childs intended nonpartisanship to accomplish, it was at least to promote, not inhibit, the "responsiveness" of the machine model to "the will" of the electorate. There are some recent empirical data indicating that the nonpartisan election is having the reverse effect.

In nonpartisan cities certain results appear to flow from the removal of regular party machinery from the local scene. Often in place of structure, continuity, and regularity is found an informal, *ad hoc,* and fluid political pattern.[64] As a consequence of this unstruc-

61. *Ibid.,* p. 130.

62. Williams and Adrian, "The Insulation of Local Politics Under the Nonpartisan Ballot," *American Political Science Review,* LII (December, 1959), 1052-63.

63. Lee, *The Politics of Nonpartisanship,* p. 102.

64. Lee's findings support this conclusion. *Ibid.,* pp. 95, 122. See also Kammerer *et al., City Managers in Politics,* pp. 85-93; and, Robert H. Salisbury and Gordon Black, "Class and Party in Partisan and

tured pattern of politics, it is frequently found, as V. O. Key found in one-party areas of the South, that elections center around personalities rather than issues. Lee found, "The only serious problem of candidate choice centers not on 'what does he stand for,' but 'what are his qualifications.' "[65]

Because of the absence of regular party machinery and the structure and continuity that it can afford, and as a result of the personality as opposed to issue politics that ensues, there is evidence that the end product is a political pattern devoid of vigorous community leadership and political responsibility.[66] As to why this situation exists, the Florida team of political scientists mentioned above concludes, "The nonpartisan election of the council seemed to us to explain the vacuum in leadership and political responsibility in so many council-manager cities."[67] Dorothy Cline in her study of Albuquerque attributes these difficulties to the fact that factions and pressure groups have been substituted for the nonexistent party organization. She asks, "How could voters hold a faction or a coalition group responsible?"[68] She adds, "The winners were responsible, if at all, to each other rather than to a political party . . . *or the voters.*"[69]

As strongly underscored in the subsection on "the problem of inconsistency," if a component of the Childs model should in actuality impair the "respon-

---

Nonpartisan Elections: The Case of Des Moines," *American Political Science Review*, LVII (September, 1963), 587.

65. Lee, *The Politics of Nonpartisanship*, p. 128.

66. Kammerer *et al.*, *City Managers in Politics*, p. 88.

67. *Ibid.*, p. 86.

68. Dorothy I. Cline, *Albuquerque and the City Manager Plan* (Albuquerque: Division of Research of the Department of Government of the University of New Mexico, 1951), p. 44.

69. *Ibid.*, (Italics mine.)

siveness'' of the mechanism to the preferences of the electorate, then Childs has become entangled in an inconsistency that strikes at the heart of his underlying values. These values envision a taut machine completely sensitized to the desires of "the people," and, according to the ideal model, nonpartisan elections are a mechanical device designed to aid the machine in reflecting these desires. However, as the above evidence suggests, it may be that nonpartisan elections in certain locales are actually dysfunctional to the operation of a governmental structure "responsive" to voter preference. If in any given situation this should prove to be the case, then Childs is confronted with a serious problem of inconsistency. For this reason, evolving empirical studies on the municipal nonpartisan election will warrant close scrutiny to ascertain how great is the difference between "the ideal" and political reality.

On one point Childs has accepted the fact that there is a variation between his ideal type and actuality. He readily acknowledges that nonpartisanship, and the manager plan generally, have resulted in the unanticipated consequence of producing an "elitist" government in many cities. Though it was never expressly stated that the model was designed to produce that result, Childs does not find this result objectionable on the grounds that the higher economic and social classes have more time to devote to service on the council, and often from these groups come the most intelligent members of the community, who will have the most talent to offer for the operation of the city. In short, Childs is accepting the political reality that, as a matter of practice but not theory, his design has tended to produce a municipal government with a patrician cast.[70] In defending his rationalistic model against this somewhat "undemocratic" development, Childs reasons that, though it may appear that the "businessmen" dominate, "be it remembered that the radical bloc gets every chance to challenge."[71] In brief, the paradigm is democratically constructed, and consequently this "undemocratic" turn of events is attributable to voter preference and not to a defective mechanism.[72]

As noted in the discussion on the politics of Dayton, Childs is unconcerned with the hypothesis that his model may have so structured access for the economic and social elites that they tend to dominate to the exclusion of other classes and groups. If this hypothesis should prove to be true, then Childs's explanation that the matter of the dominance of the elites is merely a matter of voter preference is at odds with the realities. This hypothesis is suggestive of the general tendency of Childs to separate distinctly such matters as politics, economics, and social structure. Because of this rigid categorization within his own thinking, it is possible for him to contend that even if the economic and social elites do dominate in the political sphere they do not serve merely their own political self-interests, but, in fact, represent the entire "public will." In sum, because of the separation, it is characteristic of the dominant elites in Childs's view to ignore their own economic and social interests

70. Interview with the author, January, 1964. For a conclusion, based upon empirical research, that in cities employing the nonpartisan election the major "policy forces" were "almost universally focused around the dominant social and economic classes or interests," see Kammerer *et al.*, *City Managers in Politics*, p. 88.

71. Richard S. Childs, "It's a Habit Now in Dayton," *National Municipal Review*, XXXVIII (September, 1948), 427.

72. *Ibid.*

when serving "the people" in a "political" capacity. Whether this separation generally accords with reality is questionable. That is, in the "real world" of politics, economic and social interests may be inextricably entwined with political decision-making, and, as a consequence, the governing elites may be in some situations truly "dominating" and not merely reflecting voter preference. Only continued empirical testing of the ideal model will lead to satisfactory answers to these complex and persistent questions.

The question persists as to why Childs (and the municipal reformer generally) has not adjusted his model to the empirical findings of those who are studying his schema in actual operation. Is it a personal pique and a distrust of the methodology employed? Perhaps. But for the most satisfying answer it is necessary to return again to the central theme of the preceding chapter.

Childs is impervious to subsequent empirical findings that alter the original "uncontested creed" because his system is a closed one. There is an air of unquestioned finality. The system is closed, for it lacks causal theory that would detect the need for change and, thus, allow it. Finally, in tracing down this chain reaction, Childs lacks this theory because of his view of the political and administrative worlds —a view greatly shaded by the intellectual milieu from which he sprang. His conception of these worlds is a static, formalistic, structured, and rationalistic one in which politics as a matter of process is relegated to a minor, if not nonexistent, role. Consequently, within the Childs view, studies which are preoccupied with *process* as the substance of politics, and this neatly includes all empirical research, are at best exercises in triviality, and at worst temporary distractions to the onward march of the "Unfinished Revolution."

VI

Finis

"We must cut our cloth according to the fact."
Richard S. Childs, 1914.[1]

In the preceding chapters I have outlined
Childs's construction of his machine model for municipal government. In addition, I have attempted to delineate the philosophical foundations of this model.
Finally, a critique of the Childs model was undertaken
with particular emphasis upon the fact that Childs's
system is a closed one and that this fact has profound
consequences.

In the initial section of this final chapter the question is presented as to whether Childs's ideal type has
universal validity. Childs contends that it does; the
"new" political science offers empirical studies that
suggest that in the "real municipal world" it does
not. Moreover, it is submitted in this chapter that this

1. Richard S. Childs, "The Principles Underlying the Plan," in
Commission Government with a City Manager (New York: The National
Short Ballot Organization, 1914), p. 17.

controversy over the validity of Childs's ideal type is indicative of the general need for political science to address itself in the field of urban affairs to the difficult problem of assessing and advancing our understanding of the interrelation between structure or form of municipal government and the political, social, and economic milieu in which it may be operating. This, of course, demands comparative-ecological studies, and, furthermore, it is concluded that to achieve this task of assessment and understanding it will be necessary to have dynamic rather than static models.

In the introductory chapter it was stated the underlying hypothesis of this study is that the conflict in the field of urban affairs between the "old" and "new" political sciences was a powerful one and perhaps irreconcilable. The predominant cast of this analysis centers around the nature and ramifications of this conflict. In this final chapter I conclude that a reconciliation is unlikely between Childs, as a representative of the "old" political science, and the "new" approach. Childs is unlikely to accept an empirical, comparative, and ecological approach, which is needed to develop a dynamic model, because of his conception of the worlds of politics and administration and because of his irrepressible reform zeal.

Finally, it must be stressed that, in spite of whatever "short-comings" Childs's ideal system may have, in the wake of his reformist activities has come a solid record of accomplishment. Because the focus of this study has been upon Childs as an important (perhaps the most important) representative of the "old" political science in its conflict in the study of urban politics with the newer approach, Childs's record of accomplishments has been slighted, as well as the nature of his driving and profoundly charming per‑ sonality. In the final remarks of this chapter I have attempted to correct to some extent this imbalance.

The Ideal Model: Is It Universally Valid?

Childs contends that his ideal model warrants uni‑ versal application.[2] Illustrative is his continual insis‑ tence since 1913 that the manager plan, with slight modification, is applicable to New York City, as well as to other cities.[3] The inescapable conclusion is that if the model manager design is appropriate for one of the largest cities in the world (and Childs's own "home town"), it is suitable for any sized munic‑ ipality throughout the country (and probably the world).

2. Interview with the author, January, 1964.

3. For examples over the years of Childs's recommendation of the plan for New York see *New York Times*, November 10, 1913, p. 8, col. 6, "letter to the editor"; *New York Times*, June 19, 1932, VIII, p. 3, col. 6, "City Manager Plan Advocated for Reformation of New York"; and, "New York's Mayor Must Be Three Men," *New York Times Magazine*, April 5, 1953, p. 12.

As applied to New York City, the plan provided for a single board of directors, of not over twenty-five members, elected on a nonpartisan ballot by proportional representation from the boroughs. The manager, selected by the directors, was given power to appoint and remove all department heads. There is no mayor-executive because the directors are to choose their own chairman. See Richard S. Childs, *The Charter Problem of Metropolitan Cities* (New York: Citizens Union Research Foundation, Inc., 1960), pp. 9-13. The most significant modification that Childs allowed in the case of New York was to provide for a small executive committee selected from the Board to serve as a channel for funneling policy decisions from the Board to the manager. Interview with the author, January, 1964. See also *New York Times*, June 19, 1932, VIII, p. 3, col. 6.

For the present Childs patiently accepts the "chief administrator" form of government for New York City, but he happily predicts that "New York City will fall into line sooner or later, whenever it gets mad enough." See *New York Times Magazine*, April 5, 1953, p. 12, and *New York Times*, June 19, 1932, VIII, 3, col. 6.

In contrast, though by no means recommending abolition of the manager design in toto, some commentators suggest that the Childs ideal type has greater validity for application to some political settings than to others. The debate is an old and continuing one. The first recorded evidence of it comes from the National Municipal League Convention in Dayton on November 18, 1915. At that meeting Childs implored the City Managers' Association to purge from its ranks, or in any case grant only a secondary status to, those cities that, though patterning the ideal manager model, had deviated in various ways from the "true commission-manager form of government."[4] Childs contended that such a step was essential if the "true plan" was to avoid "an undeserved bad name."[5]

These remarks brought a heated response from several managers attending the convention. Most notable was the retort from Henry M. Waite, generally considered a distinguished manager of Dayton. Bluntly Waite stated: "I sincerely regret that Mr. Childs did not take advantage of the meeting that was held by the city managers on Tuesday afternoon. If he had done so it would have been soon demonstrated to [him] the wonderful success that is being attained by city managers with varying authorities under varying charters and *under varying local conditions.*"[6] Waite concluded that he was wary of those criticisms "promulgated by people who can only approach [the prob-

4. Richard S. Childs *et al.*, "Professional Standards and Professional Ethics in the New Profession of City Manager: A Discussion," *National Municipal Review*, V (April, 1916), 196.

5. *Ibid.*

6. *Ibid.*, p. 201. (Italics mine.)

lem] from a theoretical side.'"[7] The debate had been launched.

The classic Stone, Price, and Stone study is an excellent example of this continuing conflict. Although this book generally gave approval to operation of the manager plan, it nevertheless suggests differences in degree to which actual operation approaches the model according to a typology of cities. Therefore, it is somewhat surprising that Childs should praise the book so lavishly, for the study planted seeds of doubt concerning the concept of universality of application of council-manager government. The three types— "machine cities," "faction-ridden cities," and "community-governed cities"—were developed from actual cities the authors studied and constituted evidence that cities differed as to the political environment they provided within which the plan had to operate. The authors posited the notion that these types determine the way the plan worked. For example, in the "community-governed cities" the plan functioned more nearly in accordance with expectations based on the ideal model as a result of the high degree of consensus and lack of political conflict over values and policies than in the "machine" or the "faction-ridden" ones. The authors raised such questions as "What should be the relation between the council and the city manager?" or "How much leadership should

7. *Ibid.*, p. 203. To this barb the indomitable Childs replied, "A great deal has been said about theorists this evening. I am, frankly and absolutely, a theorist, and am proud of it. . . . I suppose some of you city managers, who have just picked your way out of the shell and looked out upon the world and thought you discovered America, considered it rather an assumption for me to offer all this practical fatherly advice; but while the number of years involved are few, I want to have you know, without seeming to claim glory, that I was sawing wood on the commission-manager plan years before any of you ever heard of it." *Ibid.*, p. 209.

the manager exercise?'' In response to these queries the authors stated, ''There are no general answers to such questions, and there need not be,'' for these matters cannot be ''forced in a standardized pattern,'' but rather, will depend upon *''the variety of local conditions.''*[8]

Writers since the Stone, Price and Stone study have repeatedly suggested that the Childs ideal model has validity in an urban community with a particular political cast or style of politics. The consensus among these writers of recent years seems to be that the plan has much greater validity in the homogeneous small and medium-sized city than in the large polyglot one.[9] The most comprehensive and empirically rooted study dealing on a comparative basis with the utility of the ideal paradigm in all political settings is *The Urban Political Community*,[10] written by the authors of *City Managers in Politics*. In their field studies of ten Florida cities the researchers found two principal

8. Harold A. Stone, Don K. Price, and Kathryn H. Stone, *City Manager Government in the United States: A Review after Twenty-Five Years* (Chicago: Public Administration Service, 1940), p. 258. (Italics mine.)

9. For example, see Edward Sofen, *The Miami Metropolitan Experiment* (Bloomington, Indiana: Indiana University Press, 1963), p. 206; Karl A. Bosworth, ''The Manager *Is* a Politician,'' *Public Administration Review*, XVIII (Winter, 1958), 216-22; and S. Freedgood, ''New Strength in City Hall,'' in *The Exploding Metropolis* (Garden City, New York: Doubleday, 1958).

In fact, on the basis of the Stone, Price, and Stone studies Childs observed, ''Indeed a major lesson of these books is the advantage of having a community unified in social character, free of mutual distrust, unseparated by railroad tracks or religious or social cleavages.'' Richard S. Childs, ''The City Manager Plan Passes Its 'Exams,' '' *National Municipal Review*, XXIX (July, 1940), 444. However, Childs did not accept this point as evidence that the model be altered. On the contrary, he concludes in the same article that on the basis of their survey that ''we need [not] revise our fond *a priori* theories of yester-year!'' *Ibid.*

10. Kammerer *et al.* (Boston: Houghton Mifflin Co., 1963).

types of political styles: monopoly and competition.[11] Furthermore, they found that manager "tenure and termination" were related to the political style of a particular community. For example, they found, "Manager tenure tends to be longer in communities that have a monopolistic style of politics than in communities that have a competitive style of politics."[12] The explanation lies in the fact that "power exchanges" on the council, which can often lead to the manager's undoing and dismissal, occur with greater frequency in the fluid atmosphere of the competitive style.

In addition, the researchers found that "local-amateur city managers have a longer average tenure than outside professional managers."[13] This occurrence can be explained by the fact that the local manager is more likely to have a separate base of power from which to acquire added political security, "and perhaps most important, the local-amateur usually is found in communities which have a monopolistic style of politics, while the outsider-professional usually is found in communities that have a competitive style of politics."[14]

There is no need to reiterate all of the findings of this solidly empirical study. The crucial import of the study is its conclusion that the operation of the ideal model is dependent on the political style of the com-

11. These terms are defined as follows: "The major characteristic of monopoly politics is a lack . . . of continuing opposition from another leadership clique. Conflict prevails at a level low enough to be accommodated by the ruling clique. *Competition*, as a style of politics, exists when at least two leadership cliques compete on a *continuing* basis for elective office." Kammerer *et al.*, *The Urban Political Community*, p. 6.

12. *Ibid.*, p. 194.

13. *Ibid.*, p. 195.

14. *Ibid.*, p. 196.

munity. The model paradigm does not produce similar results in all localities, for it "must operate in *a variety of political settings,*"[15] and the effects are conditioned and tempered accordingly and they in turn affect the structure itself.

Childs, in keeping with the Taylorists' belief in the discovery of incontrovertible and universal "principles," makes only one concession in his schema to variance in political ecology, and that variable is community size. As indicated, in the case of New York City, because of its large population, he allows for an expanded council of twenty-five members with an executive committee to serve as liaison between the council and the manager. It will be recalled that Childs fervently rejected the alternative proposal of the new *Model City Charter* allowing for the popular election of the mayor-commissioner. Aberrations to accommodate alleged differences in political styles of communities are anathema to Childs.

No new theoretical premise of Childs's thought is being introduced at this point. The problem afoot here is that explored in depth in Chapter IV. Childs does not envision the variety in local political setting first suggested by Henry Waite because of his non-processual conception of "politics." He views "politics" as the same, unchanging phenomenon everywhere. Therefore, the ideal model has equal validity in all situations and for all time. The result is, as analyzed in the previous chapters, that Childs, in effect, ignores such empirical studies as *The Urban Political Community,* which tend to undermine "the uncontested creed," for they serve no useful function in his view of the political world. These studies are premised

15. *Ibid.,* p. 199. (Italics mine.)

upon "politics" as *process*. This premise Childs does not accept, and he does not accept the fruits that flow from it.

This controversy over the validity of Childs's ideal type is symptomatic of the great need in political science for extensive empirical testing of not only the council-manager model but of all forms of urban government, including the mayor-council and mayor-manager plans. What is needed are comparative-ecological studies in varying types and sizes of cities to test the interrelation between governmental structure and ecological setting. It is not a matter of "proving" the universal validity of one particular form. Rather it is a matter of assessing the effectiveness of a given structure in a particular setting. It has been previously submitted that by "effectiveness" is meant the capacity of a governmental form operating within a community to anticipate emerging problems (crime, poverty, racial strife, etc.), and to deal decisively and effectually with them before they reach crisis proportions. To state the proposition negatively, if a specific city government merely reacts to problems after they have reached the crisis stage, then one may reasonably suspect that that structure in its particular environment is "ineffective."

The variety, flux, and complexity of American urban life demands the comparative-ecological approach. Studies have already been alluded to which indicate the richness, complexity, and diversity of city politics.[16] Only a sterile political science would

16. Edward C. Banfield, *Political Influence* (Glencoe, Illinois: Free Press, 1961); Edward C. Banfield and Martin M. Meyerson, *Politics, Planning, and the Public Interest* (Glencoe, Illinois: Free Press, 1955); Robert A. Dahl, *Who Governs?* (New Haven: Yale University Press, 1961); Kammerer *et al.*, *The Urban Political Community*; Roscoe C.

attempt to make a blanket prescription of a governmental structure to fit all of the kaleidoscopic political patterns that these studies reveal. A vigorous political science, at least at present and for some time to come, must devote itself to developing the techniques and method for continued empirical and comparative research with an eye to understanding the relationship and interaction between the structure of government and its political setting.

The demand is for dynamic models rather than for rigid, static, and utopian ones. For example, in the case of the council-manager plan, after rigorous empirical research this model ought to be related to the political realities that condition it and that are in turn conditioned by the model. Illustrative is the role (or roles) of the manager in the Childs paradigm. There is a need, of course, to recognize, as Childs's model provides, that the manager is an "administrator" and to see that he is trained accordingly in all technical fields related to his areas of *expertise*. However, if, after empirical testing of the model, it is found that the manager is also involved in a political role, then a dynamic model should recognize that fact and be adjusted accordingly. To illustrate, if in fact the manager is a political creature, if he is in fact caught up in the *process* of the "authoritative allocation of values," then a dynamic model should take cognizance of that reality and the manager should be apprised accordingly and he should be prepared for the dimensions of his political roles in his formal training. At the present time this "adjustment" is

Martin *et al.*, *Decisions in Syracuse* (Bloomington, Indiana: Indiana University Press, 1961); and James Q. Wilson, *Negro Politics* (Glencoe, Illinois: Free Press, 1960).

rarely made.[17] A dynamic model would compel a reappraisal and an adjustment.

L'envoi

From the vantage point of the "new" political science, with its processual conception of the worlds of politics and administration, it may appear that Childs has not cut his "cloth according to the fact." It may be charged that he has constructed, like other traditionalist model builders, a normative model that not only has no actual existence in the "real world" of municipal government but also represents an ideal to strive for rather than a description of a set of relationships that might approach an "average" type of condition. Clearly Childs's theory is purely normative. There is no interaction of value and causal theory for the simple reason that there is an absence of causal theory. The "new" political science looks with disfavor on this lack of interaction.[18] While the

17. Typical are the course listings in the catalog for 1963-64, pages 18-19, of the Cornell University Graduate School of Business and Public Administration. The catalog sets forth "courses which should receive the student's consideration" if he is "offering" "a concentration in city management." The curriculum lists nineteen courses only one of which hints strongly at the matter of "politics." This course, entitled "Politics and Political Power," is recommended for only one term and is a broad-gauge course cutting across all levels, even the comparative international level, including socialism and communism. In short, the one course that is offered which is possibly related to "politics" probably has little to do with "the city manager in politics." The remaining eighteen courses deal with primarily "technical" matters—they relate to the model role of the manager as "administrator." Illustrative are the following course titles: Governmental Accounting, Public Personnel Management, Legal Aspects of Planning, Traffic Engineering, Municipal Sanitation, Taxation, and courses of a similar nature pertaining to matters of "management" and "administration."

18. For example, see David Easton, *The Political System* (New York: Alfred A. Knopf, 1960).

"behavioral persuasion" pursues empirical, comparative, ecological, and nomothetic research in the hope
of developing a verifiable political science in urban
politics, Childs indefatigably carries on the "Unfinished Revolution."

This chasm between the "new" and the "old"
political sciences is deep, and the differences between
these schools show up clearly in the field of urban
affairs because so much recent research has centered
on this area of interest, for a variety of reasons.
These differences stem from differing conceptions of
the nature of politics and administration—one processual and one nonprocessual. However, in Childs's case
there is one added nuance that perpetuates the cleavage and makes unlikely any reconciliation.

This added factor is Childs's insatiable zeal for
reform. He is a master reformer from an era in which
good reformers were a commonplace. Possessed of the
Progressive's utter detestation for the politicos who
in Childs's early years had permeated urban politics,
he is consumed with the passion for reform. He constructs his model of municipal government for solely
one purpose—to waylay the spoilsmen.

This fervor remains undiminished to this day. The
undercurrent of a militant reformism can be sensed
in Childs's description of current activities at the
National Municipal League Office: "There come to our
office, by letter or in person every week, the spokesmen
of local discontent, usually little people, unimportant
people, novices in their local political arena, green at
their self-imposed assignment of 'having to do something about it,' but they are the salt of the earth for
they start out toward seemingly sure defeat and they

carry courage in their hands.'"[19] Childs continues to use, metaphorically, the language of the battlefield. In recent reference to the League's propaganda materials he speaks of "our superb arsenal," and the members of the League of Women Voters, who have afforded great assistance in the manager movement, are referred to as the "front-line troops." Finally, he exclaims, "Do not conclude that this war is over because of our many civic victories. On the contrary 'there is beautiful fighting ahead.' "[20]

In view of this unabating revolutionary ardor, coupled with the more fundamental problem of Childs's perception of the nature of politics and administration, one would be failing to cut the "cloth according to the fact" to expect Childs to "adjust" his ideal paradigm to the "political realities." To speak to the revolutionary of a need for the "revision" of doctrine to bring it in accord with the "reality" is irritating at best and quite likely is to give him hint of subversion. To prescribe an "alteration" in the reformer's ideal type is to infer that his program was ill-conceived or imperfectly designed at the outset. Such inferences Childs adamantly resists, and, the more intensely he opposes, the greater grows the division between him and the "new" political science.

Childs is aware of this split, but he is unconcerned. He is convinced of the righteousness of his cause, and he is supremely confident of ultimate and total victory. To me Childs exclaimed, "I admit cheerfully that I am prejudiced. You young political scientists can af-

19. Richard S. Childs, "Civic Victories in the United States," *National Municipal Review*, XXXXIV (September, 1955), 399.
20. *Ibid.*, p. 401.

ford to be neutral because of what the old generation has accomplished in the field of urban affairs.'"[21]

What has the manager movement "accomplished"? On a quantitative basis Childs has reason to look with pride on the growth of his "brain child." At the present time over eighteen hundred American cities, which includes over forty-three million American citizens, have adopted the manager plan since the first skirmish at Sumter, and, with customary gusto, Childs notes, "Projecting the current rate of adoptions, we can forecast the plan as due to be approximately unanimous in another twenty years!"[22]

Even by the most rigorous objective standard, there is also a solid qualitative record of achievement. From the viewpoint of a supposedly civilized and democratic society, there were, in Childs's formative years, sordid conditions existing in many American cities (not to mention Childs's New York City) ranging from boodling to child prostitution. Though businessmen proponents might stress only the "evils" of high taxes, poor services, waste, and general inefficiency, the manager movement, under the guiding hand of Childs, had a broader basis of reform aimed at all of these insidious practices.

It would not accord with the facts to suggest that the manager movement has brought the millenium to urban politics by eradicating all iniquities, but it would be remiss to fail to note that in addition to helping eliminate many of these conditions by bringing a heightened sense of *expertise,* integrity, and commitment to municipal service (hardly classifiable as

21. Interview with the author, 1964.
22. Richard S. Childs, "The Coming of the Council-Manager Plan," February 21, 1963, p. 11 (mimeographed).

"bad" qualities), the movement assisted in bringing about, initially at least, an intensified interest in enlightened citizen involvement in municipal affairs. From those who hold democratic values, these results should rate high marks.

The adjective "enlightened" is appropriate. Though Childs, in harmony with the impact of Progressivism and Taylorism upon his thinking, strongly promotes "efficiency" in municipal government, this fact must not lead to the assumption that Childs views the scope of city government with the myopia of a reactionary businessman. Childs, with the warmth and vision of his Progressive roots fully exposed, has an infinitely broader perspective than this, as the following comment made in 1917 will reveal (again, it is Dayton that serves as the model):

After you have got the politicians out of the city hall, after government ceases to mean a parcel of jobs to be contested for, after you have developed a public agency sensitive to the desires of the electorate and at the same time efficient and clean in administration; then what? The city having obtained at last a first class auto instead of a stagecoach, where shall we drive? Does it mean merely a lower tax rate? Dayton is just beginning to answer that question by exhibiting a government which delights in undertaking high social service. Here is a city government which is beginning to undertake the responsibility of looking after the people of the city. It frankly and definitely proposes to abolish private charity within the city by gradually taking over every tested and necessary philanthropy. It tries to do something about the cost of living. It reduces infant mortality 40%. It undertakes to restore human derelicts. It develops wholesome occupation for children in little farm gardens. It abandons the laissez faire policy and assumes responsibility for trying to make Dayton a nice place to live in. . . . Dayton seems likely to show *how much, in human terms rather than in financial statistics, good government means.*

The other commission-manager cities are still busy cleaning house, getting their finances in order, catching up with their public works problem, repairing old neglect. When they get this done, what will they do? Gild the dome on the city hall? Or will they call in the social worker and follow up their surveys of the administration by surveys of the people in the alleys? We know at least that Dayton, the pioneer city, is leading in the right direction. . . .[23]

In an interview with me in January, 1964, Childs reaffirmed his commitment to this specific statement. Whether the Childs machine model is producing or is capable of producing these avowed ends, raises again "the problem of inconsistency," and the concomitant problem of possible incongruities between "the ideal model and political reality." These matters have already received their due. Even if the means prescribed are inadequate to the task, this possibility does not detract from the enlightened vision that Childs has for America's cities.

Finally, recognition must be given Childs for his accomplishment through the short ballot and council-manager movements of articulating the importance of institutional-structural arrangements. Initially at least, Childs perceived that structure affected "access" to the loci of political power in urban affairs. He realized that "bossism" thrived on the decentralized structural forms of government ("ramshackle government," as he called it) commonplace in American cities and counties. Childs sought to manipulate the structure so as to deny access to the boss and to

23. Richard S. Childs, "How the Commission-Manager Plan Is Getting Along," *National Municipal Review,* VI (January, 1917), 70. (Italics mine.)

facilitate access for the "good government forces." Childs may be in error in contending that his structural arrangement is the *only* answer, but he scores high in perceiving initially the relationship between structure and function.

This study has been concerned with matters of models, and method and elements of this genre; in sum, with political science. Under the heavy hand of the political scientist, the poetical always fares poorly. My subject is a man of incomparable wit, charm, and ebullience—all of these endearing qualities had to be slighted in this appraisal. This is regrettable, for as one writer stated the matter on Childs's eightieth birthday, "At no age was he a common man; at 80 he remains one of a kind. . . ."[24] With this I fully agree, and I predict he will keep students of the urban scene busy for some years to come.

24. *New York Times*, May 24, 1962, p. 34, col. 2.

Bibliography

Books

Banfield, Edward C. *Political Influence.* Glencoe, Illinois: Free Press, 1961.

Banfield, Edward C., and Meyerson, Martin M. *Politics, Planning, and the Public Interest.* Glencoe, Illinois: Free Press, 1955.

Banfield, Edward C., and Wilson, James Q. *City Politics.* Cambridge: Harvard and M.I.T. Presses, 1963.

Barnard, Chester I. *The Functions of the Executive.* Cambridge: Harvard University Press, 1961.

Bentley, Arthur F. *The Process of Government.* Bloomington, Indiana: Principia Press, 1949.

Berelson, B. R., *et al. Voting.* Chicago: University of Chicago Press, 1954.

Bryce, James. *The American Commonwealth.* Vol. I. New York: The Macmillan Co., 1897.

Burdick, Eugene, and Brodbeck, Arthur C. (eds.). *American Voting Behavior.* Glencoe, Illinois: Free Press, 1959.

Campbell, Angus, *et al. The American Voter.* New York: Wiley, 1960.

Chalmers, David M. *The Social and Political Ideas of the Muckrakers.* New York: The Citadel Press, 1964.

Childs, Richard S. *Civic Victories: The Story of an Unfinished Revolution.* New York: Harper and Brothers, 1952.

———. *Short Ballot Principles.* Boston: Houghton Mifflin Co., 1911.

———. *William Hamlin Childs.* Privately printed, 1957.

Cline, Dorothy I. *Albuquerque and the City Manager Plan.* Albuquerque: Division of Research of the Department of Government of the University of New Mexico, 1951.

Commager, Henry Steele. *The American Mind.* New Haven: Yale University Press, 1950.

Conway, M. D. (ed.). *The Writings of Thomas Paine.* Vol. I. New York: G. P. Putnam's Sons, 1894.

Dahl, Robert A. *Who Governs?* New Haven: Yale University Press, 1961.

Easton, David. *The Political System.* New York: Alfred A. Knopf, 1960.

Etzioni, Amitai. *A Comparative Analysis of Complex Organizations.* Glencoe, Illinois: Free Press, 1961.

Eulau, Heinz. *The Behavioral Persuasion in Politics.* New York: Random House, 1963.

Filler, Louis. *Crusaders for American Liberalism.* New York: Crowell-Collier Publishing Co., 1961.

Flynn, Edward J. *You're the Boss.* New York: The Viking Press, 1947.

Frost, Richard T. (ed.). *Cases in State and Local Government.* Englewood Cliffs, New Jersey: Prentice-Hall, 1961.

Gabriel, Ralph H. *The Course of American Democratic Thought.* 2d ed. New York: Ronald Press Co., 1956.

Gaus, John M. *Reflections on Public Administration.* University, Alabama: University of Alabama Press, 1947.

Gilbertson, H. S. *The County: The Dark Continent of American Politics.* New York: The National Short Ballot Organization, 1917.

Golembiewski, Robert T. *Behavior and Organization: O & M and the Small Group.* Chicago: Rand McNally and Co., 1962.

Goodnow, Frank. *Politics and Administration.* New York: The Macmillan Co., 1900.

Gross, Neal, *et al. Explorations in Role Analysis: Studies of the School Superintendency Role.* New York: John Wiley and Sons, Inc., 1958.

Gulick, Luther, and Urwick, Lyndall (eds.). *Papers on the Science of Administration.* New York: Institute of Public Administration, 1937.

Harder, Marvin A. *Nonpartisan Elections: A Political Illusion?* New York: Holt, 1958.

Hofstadter, Richard. *Social Darwinism in American Thought.* Boston: The Beacon Press, 1955.

———. *The Age of Reform: From Bryan to F. D. R.* New York: Vintage Books, Inc., 1960.

Kales, Albert M. *Unpopular Government in the United States.* Chicago: University of Chicago Press, 1914.

Kammerer, Gladys M., Farris, Charles D., DeGrove, John M., and Clubok, Alfred B. *City Managers in Politics.* Gainesville, Florida: University of Florida Press, 1962.

———. *The Urban Political Community.* Boston: Houghton Mifflin Co., 1963.

Key, V. O. *Southern Politics.* New York: Alfred A. Knopf, 1949.

Lasswell, Harold D. *Politics, Who Gets What, When, How.* New York: McGraw-Hill, 1936.

Lazarsfeld, P. F., *et al. The People's Choice.* 2d ed. New York: Columbia University Press, 1948.

Lee, Eugene C. *The Politics of Nonpartisanship.* Berkeley: University of California Press, 1960.

Levin, Murray B. *The Alienated Voter.* New York: Holt, Rinehart, and Winston, Inc., 1960.

Link, Arthur S. *Wilson: The Road to the White House.* Princeton, New Jersey: Princeton University Press, 1947.

March, James G., and Simon, Herbert A. *Organizations.* New York: John Wiley and Sons, Inc., 1958.

Martin, Roscoe C., *et al. Decisions in Syracuse.* Bloomington, Indiana: Indiana University Press, 1961.

Municipal Yearbook. Chicago: International City Managers' Association, 1934-to date.

Myers, Gustavus. *The History of Tammany Hall.* New York: Boni and Liveright, Inc., 1917.

National Municipal League. *Model City Charter.* New York: National Municipal League, 1941, 1963.

National Municipal League. *Model City Charter* (Draft of Commentary). New York: National Municipal League, 1963.

National Municipal League. *Model City Charter* (Tentative Draft). New York: National Municipal League, 1963.

Patton, Clifford W. *The Battle for Municipal Reform.* Washington, D. C.: American Council on Public Affairs, 1940.

Regier, C. C. *The Era of the Muckrakers.* Chapel Hill: University of North Carolina Press, 1932.

Rice, Stuart A. *Quantitative Methods in Politics.* New York: Alfred A. Knopf, 1928.

Ridley, Clarence E. *The Role of the City Manager in Policy Formulation.* Chicago: International City Managers' Association, 1950.

Ridley, Clarence E., and Nolting, Orin F. *The City-Manager Profession.* Chicago: University of Chicago Press, 1934.

Roethlisberger, F. J., and Dickson, W. J. *Management and the Worker.* Cambridge: Harvard University Press, 1939.

Schattschneider, E. E. *The Semi-Sovereign People.* New York: Holt, Rinehart and Winston, 1960.

Schubert, Glendon. *The Public Interest: A Critique of the Theory of a Political Concept.* Glencoe, Illinois: Free Press, 1960.

Simon, Herbert. *Administrative Behavior.* New York: The Macmillan Co., 1957.

Sofen, Edward. *The Miami Metropolitan Experiment.* Bloomington, Indiana: Indiana University Press, 1963.

Stewart, Frank M. *A Half Century of Municipal Reform: The History of the National Municipal League.* Berkeley: University of California Press, 1950.

Stone, Harold A., Price, Don K., and Stone, Kathryn H. *City Manager Government in Nine Cities.* Chicago: Public Administration Service, 1940.

————. *City Manager Government in the United States: A Review after Twenty-Five Years.* Chicago: Public Administration Service, 1940.

Straetz, Ralph A. *PR Politics in Cincinnati.* New York: New York University Press, 1958.

Taft, Charles P. *City Management: The Cincinnati Experiment.* New York: Farrar and Rinehart, 1933.

Taylor, Frederick W. *The Principles of Scientific Management.* New York: Harper and Brothers, 1911.

The Short Ballot Bulletin. New York: The National Short Ballot Organization, 1911-1920.

Thompson, Victor. *Modern Organization.* New York: Alfred A. Knopf, 1961.

Truman, David B. *The Governmental Process.* New York: Alfred A. Knopf, 1951.

Waldo, Dwight. *The Administrative State.* New York: Ronald Press Co., 1948.

Weber, G. A. *Organized Efforts for the Improvement of Methods of Administration in the United States.* New York: Brookings Institute, 1919.

Weber, Max. *Theory of Social and Economic Organization* (trans. A. M. Henderson and T. Parsons). New York: Oxford University Press, 1947.

White, Leonard D. *The City Manager.* Chicago: University of Chicago Press, 1927.

Wiebe, Robert H. *Businessmen and Reform.* Cambridge: Harvard University Press, 1962.

Willoughby, W. F. *The Government of Modern States.* New York: D. Appleton-Century Co., 1919.

Wilson, James Q. *Negro Politics.* Glencoe, Illinois: Free Press, 1960.

Wilson, Woodrow. *The New Freedom.* New York: Doubleday, Page and Co., 1913.

Articles and Periodicals

Adrian, Charles R. "A Study of Three Communities," *Public Administration Review*, XVIII (Spring, 1958), 208-13.

———. "A Typology for Nonpartisan Elections," *Western Political Quarterly*, XII (June, 1959), 449-58.

American Political Science Association. "Toward a More Responsible Two-Party System," *American Political Science Review* (Supplement), XXXXIV (September, 1950).

Beard, Charles A. "Politics and City Government," *National Municipal Review*, VI (March, 1917), 205-10.

———. "The Ballot's Burden," *Political Science Quarterly*, XXIV (December, 1909), 589-614.

Bosworth, Karl A. "The Manager *Is* a Politician," *Public Administration Review*, XVIII (Winter, 1958), 216-22.

Childs, Richard S. "Along the Governmental Battle Front," *National Municipal Review*, XIX (January, 1930), 5-6.

———. "A New Civic Army," *National Municipal Review*, X (June, 1921), 327-30.

———. "A Theoretically Perfect County," *The Annals of the American Academy of Political and Social Science*, XXXXVII (May, 1913), 274-78.

———. "Ballot Is Still Too Long," *National Municipal Review*, XXXV (February, 1946), 67-70.

———. "Best States for a Murder," October, 1963 (mimeographed).

———. "Citizen Organization for Control of Government," *The Annals of the American Academy of Political and Social Science*, CCLXXXXII (March, 1954), 129-35.

———. "City Manager Government," *National Municipal Review*, XXV (February, 1936), 50-51.

———. "Civic Victories in the United States," *National Municipal Review*, XXXXIV (September, 1955), 398-402.

———. "Council-Manager Cities 1,000 Strong," *American City*, LXVI (January, 1951), 69-70.

————. "County Manager Plan," *American City* (Town and Country Ed.), XI (December, 1914), 457-61.

————. "Democracy That Might Work," *Century*, CXX (January, 1930), 11-17.

————. "Fifteenth Annual Report of the Guest Artist," November, 1962 (typed manuscript).

————. "500 'Non-Political' Elections," *National Municipal Review*, XXXVIII (June, 1949), 278-82.

————. "Half Century of Municipal Reform," *American Journal of Economics and Sociology*, XV (April, 1956), 321-26.

————. "How the Commission-Manager Plan Is Getting Along," *National Municipal Review*, IV (July, 1915), 371-82.

————. "How the Commission-Manager Plan Is Getting Along," *National Municipal Review*, VI (January, 1917), 69-73.

————. "How to Work for Charter Reform," *American City*, VIII (February, 1913), 149-50.

————. "It's a Habit Now in Dayton," *National Municipal Review*, XXXVIII (September, 1948), 421-27.

————. "League's Second Stretch," *National Municipal Review*, XXXIII (November, 1944), 514-19.

————. "Lockport Proposal to Improve the Commission Plan," *American City*, IV (June, 1911), 285-87.

————. "New York's Mayor Must Be Three Men," *New York Times Magazine* (April 5, 1953), 12-13.

————. "No Tenure for City Managers," *National Municipal Review*, XXXVIII (April, 1949), 167-70.

————. "Non-Partisan Elections in 14 Unwieldy Constituencies," 1964 (mimeographed).

————. "Peanut Politics and the Short Ballot," *Harper's Weekly*, LVIII (October 25, 1913), 22-23.

————. "Politics Without Politicians," *The Saturday Evening Post*, CLXXXII (January 22, 1910), 5-6, 35.

————. "Quest for Leadership," *National Civic Review*, L (November, 1961), 526-29.

——. "Ramshackle County Government," *Outlook,* CXIII (May 3, 1916), 39-45.

——. "Rise and Spread of the City Manager Plan of Local Government," *American City,* XXXXIII (September, 1930), 131-32.

——. "Separate Election of Mayors in Council-Manager Plan," 1963 (mimeographed).

——. "Short Ballot and the Commission Plan," *The Annals of the American Academy of Political and Social Science,* XXXVIII (November, 1911), 148-51.

——. "State Manager Plan," *National Municipal Review,* VI (November, 1917), 659-63.

——. "The Best Practice Under the City-Manager Plan," *National Municipal Review,* XXII (January, 1933), 41-44.

——. "The City Manager Plan Passes Its 'Exams,'" *National Municipal Review,* XXIX (July, 1940), 443-47.

——. "The City Manager Plan Will Endure," *American City,* LV (May, 1940), 35-36.

——. "The Coming of the Council-Manager Plan," February 21, 1963 (mimeographed).

——. "The Enduring Qualities of a Successful Manager," *Public Management,* XXXXV (January, 1963), 2-4.

——. "The League's Second Stretch," *National Municipal Review,* XXXIII (November, 1944), 514-19.

——. "The Lockport Proposal," *American City,* IV (June, 1911), 285-287.

——. "The New Opportunity for the City Manager Plan," *National Municipal Review,* XXII (January, 1933), 593-95.

——. "The Principles Underlying the Plan," in *Commission Government with a City Manager.* New York: The National Short Ballot Organization, 1914.

——. "The Rise and Spread of the City Manager Plan," *American City,* XXXXIII (September, 1930), 131-32.

——. "The Short Ballot," *Outlook,* LXXXXII (July, 1909), 635-39.

——. "The Theory of the New Controlled-Executive

Plan," *National Municipal League,* II (January, 1913), 76-81.

———. "Theories of Responsive Government Prove Practical," *Public Management,* XXIX (December, 1947), 353-57.

———. "Twelfth Annual Report of the Guest Artist," November, 1959 (typed manuscript).

———. "Use of the Word 'Mayor' in the Model City Charter," 1963 (typed manuscript).

———. "What a Democracy Would Be Like," *Everybody's,* XXVI (March, 1912), 372-73.

———. "What Ails Pittsburgh?" *American City,* III (July, 1910), 9-12.

———. "What the City Manager of Klebubudaydoc Did," in the *City Manager Association Yearbook.* Clarksburg, West Virginia: City Manager Association, 1921.

———. "What to Expect of Political Reform," *National Municipal Review,* XXI (June, 1932), 349-53.

———. "Woodrow Wilson Legacy," *National Municipal Review,* XXXXVI (January, 1957), 14-19.

Childs, Richard S., *et al.* "Professional Standards and Professional Ethics in the New Profession of City Manager: A Discussion," *National Municipal Review,* V (April, 1916), 195-210.

Committee Report, "Suggested Procedure for Selecting a City Manager," *National Municipal Review* (Supplement), XXII (December, 1933).

Dahl, Robert A. "The Behavioral Approach," *American Political Science Review,* LV (December, 1961), 763-72.

———. "The Science of Public Administration: Three Problems," *Public Administration Review,* VII (Winter, 1947), 1-11.

Freedgood, S. "New Strength in City Hall," in *The Exploding Metropolis.* Garden City, New York: Doubleday, 1958.

Herson, Lawrence J. R. "The Lost World of Municipal

Government," *American Political Science Review,* LI (June, 1957), 330-45.

Kammerer, Gladys M. "Is the Manager a Political Leader? —Yes," *Public Management,* XXXXIV (February, 1962), 26-29.

——. "Role Diversity of City Managers," *Administrative Science Quarterly,* VIII (March, 1964), 421-42.

Merton, Robert K. "The Functions of the Political Machine," in Ulmer, Sidney (ed.). *Introductory Readings in Political Behavior.* Chicago: Rand McNally and Co., 1961.

Mooney, James D. "The Principles of Organization," in Gulick, Luther, and Urwick, Lyndall (eds.). *Papers on the Science of Administration.* New York: Institute of Public Administration, 1937.

Pfiffner, John M. "Policy Leadership—For What?" *Public Administration Review,* XIX (Winter, 1959), 121-24.

Price, Don K. "The Promotion of the Council-Manager Plan," *Public Opinion Quarterly,* V (1941), 563-78.

Salisbury, Robert H., and Black, Gordon. "Class and Party in Partisan and Nonpartisan Elections: The Case of Des Moines," *American Political Science Review,* LVII (September, 1963), 584-92.

Sayre, Wallace S. "The General Manager Idea for Large Cities," *Public Administration Review,* XIV (Spring, 1954), 253-58.

"The Idea Grew," *National Municipal Review,* XL (January, 1951), 63.

Urwick, Lyndall. "Executive Decentralization with Functional Co-ordination," *Public Administration Review,* XIII (Spring, 1935), 344-50.

——. "Organization as a Technical Problem," in Gulick, Luther, and Urwick, Lyndall (eds.). *Papers on the Science of Administration.* New York: Institute of Public Administration, 1937.

White, Andrew. *Forum,* X (December, 1890), 25-30.

Williams, Oliver P., and Adrian, Charles R. "The Insulation of Local Politics Under the Nonpartisan Ballot,"

American Political Science Review, LII (December, 1959), 1052-63.

Willoughby, Alfred. "R. S. Childs," no date (mimeographed).

Wilson, James Q. "Manager Under Fire," in Frost, Richard T. (ed.). *Cases in State and Local Government.* Englewood Cliffs, New Jersey: Prentice-Hall, 1961.

Wilson, Woodrow. "Hide-and-Seek Politics," *North American Review*, CXCI (May, 1910). 585-601.

———. "The Study of Administration," *Political Science Quarterly*, II (June, 1887), 197-222.

Pamphlet Materials

Childs, Richard S. *A Suggestion for an Optional Second Class Cities Law.* New York: n.p., n.d., 31 pp.

———. *The Charter Problem of Metropolitan Cities.* New York: Citizens Union Research Foundation, Inc., 1960, 19 pp.

———. *The Story of the Short Ballot Cities.* New York: The National Short Ballot Organization, 1914, 20 pp.

Childs, Richard S., *et al. Best Practice with the Manager Plan.* New York: National Municipal League, 1963, 20 pp.

The City Manager's Code of Ethics. Chicago: International City Managers' Association, 1963, 1 p.

The Story of the Council-Manager Plan. New York: National Municipal League, 1962, 32 pp.

Newspapers

New York Times, 1913-1964.

Other Sources

The Childs Files in the Office of the National Municipal League.

The Childs Papers on the National Short Ballot Organization. Cornell University Graduate School of Business and Public Administration. Catalog for 1963-1964.

Interview with Richard S. Childs by the author. January, 1964.

Letters to the author. From Richard S. Childs: October 22, 1963; March 10, 1964. From Herbert Emmerich: January 13, 1964.

Library of Congress Materials. Memorandum, September 28, 1909, 3 pp; Minutes of meeting of Executive Board of Short Ballot Organization, September 23, 1909, 3 pp; and "Progress Report No. 1," September 23, 1909, Richard S. Childs, 4 pp. In the Wilson Papers, Series VI, File 1122, there are: Childs to Wilson, July 24, 1913, 2 pp; Childs to Wilson, October 6, 1913, 2 pp; W. H. Childs to Wilson, February 7, 1914, 1 p; R. S. Childs to Wilson, October 20, 1915, 1 p; Wilson to Childs, October 22, 1915, 1 p; Childs to Wilson, January 7, 1915, 1 p; Memorandum by Wilson, January 11, 1915, 1 p; and Childs to Advisory Board, April 12, 1920, 2 pp.

Index